PayPal APIs: Up and Running

PayPal APIs: Up and Running

Michael Balderas

Beijing · Cambridge · Farnham · Köln · Sebastopol · Tokyo

PayPal APIs: Up and Running

by Michael Balderas

Copyright © 2011 O'Reilly Media, Inc. All rights reserved.
Printed in the United States of America.

Published by O'Reilly Media, Inc., 1005 Gravenstein Highway North, Sebastopol, CA 95472.

O'Reilly books may be purchased for educational, business, or sales promotional use. Online editions are also available for most titles (*http://my.safaribooksonline.com*). For more information, contact our corporate/institutional sales department: (800) 998-9938 or *corporate@oreilly.com*.

Editor: Mary Treseler	**Indexer:** Angela Howard
Production Editor: Kristen Borg	**Cover Designer:** Karen Montgomery
Copyeditor: Genevieve d'Entremont	**Interior Designer:** David Futato
Proofreader: Kristen Borg	**Illustrator:** Robert Romano

Printing History:

February 2011:   First Edition.

ISBN: 978-1-449-39612-1

[LSI]

1297349459

Table of Contents

Preface

Virtually every application delivery model is experiencing a surging demand for transaction convenience. In this book, I introduce PayPal APIs, along with instructions and resources for their integration in different environments, including websites and mobile applications.

Goals of This Book

The goal of this book is to help you understand what PayPal has to offer. Let's face it, you want to get money from your customers into your bank account as quickly as possible, and I want to help you accomplish this. By the end of this book, you will have a better understanding of what PayPal is, how PayPal can streamline your payments, and how to get the most out of PayPal for your particular payment situation.

Who Should Read This Book

This book is for anyone who wants to accept payments for their goods or services through PayPal. You might be an individual with an open source project looking to accept donations, a multimillion-dollar corporation, a nonprofit requesting donations to help a cause, or a software developer writing mobile apps for cell phones. PayPal can provide you with solutions, no matter who you are. The code samples in this book are provided in PHP and Objective-C, and limited code coverage of Droid is included in Chapter 5. An understanding of using APIs is recommended, but not required.

How This Book Is Organized

Here is a brief summary of the chapters in the book and what you can expect from each:

Chapter 1, The PayPal API
> Covers the PayPal API and how to start using it to accept payments, with an emphasis on choosing an integration method for your project as well as obtaining the necessary credentials to get started. I also cover how to use the sandbox to test your application.

Chapter 2, PayPal Express Checkout
> Covers Express Checkout and how to use the API to execute Express Checkout Payments. This chapter contrasts the Generic (or Traditional) checkout workflow with the Express Checkout workflow. All four of the Express Checkout operations (`SetExpressCheckout`, `GetExpressCheckoutDetails`, `DoExpressCheckoutPayment`, and `Callback`) are covered.

Chapter 3, PayPal Website Payments Pro
> Covers Website Payments Pro, with an emphasis on Direct Payments. I demonstrate the Direct Payment workflow in a sample transaction. A simple Direct Payment Integration sample is also included.

Chapter 4, PayPal Adaptive Payments
> Covers Adaptive Payments, including an overview of Adaptive Payments as well as a breakdown of the Permission Levels provided via Adaptive Payments. Application workflows, Payment Approval, and Payment flows are also included.

Chapter 5, PayPal Mobile Express Checkout
> Covers Mobile Checkout, with an emphasis on the newly released Mobile Express Checkout and the Mobile Payment Libraries for iOS- and Droid-based smartphones.

Conventions Used in This Book

The following typographical conventions are used in this book:

Italic
> Indicates new terms, URLs, email addresses, filenames, and file extensions.

`Constant width`
> Used for program listings, as well as within paragraphs to refer to program elements such as variable or function names, databases, data types, environment variables, statements, and keywords.

`Constant width bold`
> Shows commands or other text that should be typed literally by the user.

Constant width italic

Shows text that should be replaced with user-supplied values or by values determined by context.

This icon signifies a tip, suggestion, or general note.

This icon indicates a warning or caution.

Using Code Examples

This book is here to help you get your job done. In general, you may use the code in this book in your programs and documentation. You do not need to contact us for permission unless you're reproducing a significant portion of the code. For example, writing a program that uses several chunks of code from this book does not require permission. Selling or distributing a CD-ROM of examples from O'Reilly books does require permission. Answering a question by citing this book and quoting example code does not require permission. Incorporating a significant amount of example code from this book into your product's documentation does require permission.

We appreciate, but do not require, attribution. An attribution usually includes the title, author, publisher, and ISBN. For example: "*PayPal APIs: Up and Running* by Michael Balderas. Copyright 2011 O'Reilly Media, Inc., 978-1-449-39612-1."

If you feel your use of code examples falls outside fair use or the permission given here, feel free to contact us at *permissions@oreilly.com.*

Safari® Books Online

Safari Books Online is an on-demand digital library that lets you easily search over 7,500 technology and creative reference books and videos to find the answers you need quickly.

With a subscription, you can read any page and watch any video from our library online. Read books on your cell phone and mobile devices. Access new titles before they are available for print, and get exclusive access to manuscripts in development and post feedback for the authors. Copy and paste code samples, organize your favorites, download chapters, bookmark key sections, create notes, print out pages, and benefit from tons of other time-saving features.

O'Reilly Media has uploaded this book to the Safari Books Online service. To have full digital access to this book and others on similar topics from O'Reilly and other publishers, sign up for free at *http://my.safaribooksonline.com*.

How to Contact Us

Please address comments and questions concerning this book to the publisher:

O'Reilly Media, Inc.
1005 Gravenstein Highway North
Sebastopol, CA 95472
800-998-9938 (in the United States or Canada)
707-829-0515 (international or local)
707 829-0104 (fax)

We have a web page for this book, where we list errata, examples, and any additional information. You can access this page at:

http://oreilly.com/catalog/0636920014386

To comment or ask technical questions about this book, send email to:

bookquestions@oreilly.com

For more information about our books, courses, conferences, and news, see our website at *http://www.oreilly.com*.

Find us on Facebook: *http://facebook.com/oreilly*

Follow us on Twitter: *http://twitter.com/oreillymedia*

Watch us on YouTube: *http://www.youtube.com/oreillymedia*

CHAPTER 1

The PayPal API

Overview of the PayPal API

PayPal provides developer access to its payments system via its Name-Value Pair API, referred to as NVP API for the remainder of this book. The NVP API allows a merchant to access PayPal and accomplish the following tasks:

- Accept PayPal during your checkout process via Express Checkout
- Charge a credit card during a Direct Payment session
- Capture previously authorized Express Checkout and Direct Payment payments
- Reauthorize or void previous authorizations
- Pay single or multiple recipients via Mass Payment
- Issue full refunds or multiple partial refunds
- Search transactions using a specified search criteria
- Retrieve details of a specific transaction
- Accept PayPal for multiparty payments
- Accept PayPal for subscriptions or freemium models. (Freemium models offer a basic product or service free of charge, while charging a premium for advanced features. A good example is something like CCleaner: you can download it and use it free, and pay for a license if you want support. You can also make donations to future development—and they accept PayPal for both.)

PayPal's NVP API makes it simple to integrate PayPal payments into your specific web application. You, the merchant, construct an NVP string and post it via HTTPS (HTTP Secure, aka TLS/SSL) to the PayPal authorization server. PayPal posts back an NVP-formatted response that you then parse in your web application for the information relevant to the payment. Figure 1-1 shows a basic request and response workflow.

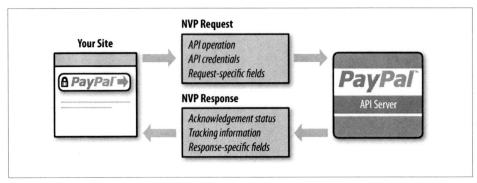

Figure 1-1. Basic NVP request and response

The request identifies:

- The name or method of the API operation to be performed and its version
- PayPal API credentials
- Operation-specific parameters formatted as name/value pairs

 Adaptive APIs also require an APP ID during the request.

The PayPal API server executes the operation and returns a response containing:

- Acknowledgment of success or failure (including any warnings returned in case of failure)
- PayPal tracking information specific to the API operation
- Response-specific information required to fulfill the request

Some features of the NVP API, such as Express Checkout, require calls to multiple API operations. Other APIs like Direct Pay only require one call. But typically, you are required to:

1. Call an API operation—for example, SetExpressCheckout—that sets up the return URL PayPal uses to redirect your buyer's browser after the buyer finishes on PayPal. Other setup routines can be performed by this same API operation.
2. Call additional API operations after receiving the buyer's permission on PayPal, such as GetExpressCheckoutDetails or DoExpressCheckoutPayment.

Figure 1-2 shows the execution workflow between your application and PayPal.

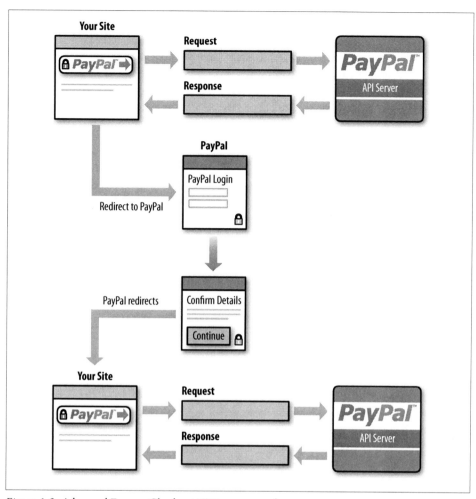

Figure 1-2. Advanced Express Checkout NVP request and response

Getting Started

There are two methods for integrating PayPal's NVP API into your application: direct integration and integration through a Software Development Kit (referred to as SDK). I focus on direct integration into your website and applications.

Direct Versus SDK Integration

Direct integration allows you to use the programming language of your choice to communicate via the NVP API. This is the most flexible approach and allows direct access to the Name-Value Pair elements of the API. SDK integration provides simple functions for integration using the NVP API. There are SDKs are provided for Java, ASP.NET, PHP, Coldfusion, and Ruby. This type of integration typically wraps the HTTPS interfaces in the respective language, making the operations more natural for the developer to work with, because they are formatted in a familiar language and require just a few simple function calls to access.

Testing Versus Live Implementation

PayPal provides a sandbox environment to use while developing your application. The environment replicates the live environment, but true payment processing doesn't occur when using the sandbox. Once you have fully developed and debugged your application, you can then switch to the live environment and start taking payments. Switching between the two is as simple as changing the target server and the API credentials used to access the server. The rest of your application will remain unchanged.

I recommend setting up your API credentials in separate files within your application. This way, you can have your sandbox credentials in one file and your production credentials in another file, referenced accordingly. For added security, I would locate these files on your server outside the default webroot, so that they cannot be called directly from the web browser.

Obtaining API Credentials

To access the NVP API, you first need to establish credentials. These identify who you are and ensure payments get to where they need to go. You establish credentials through either an API signature or an API certificate. You will need two sets of API credentials: one for development and one for production.

Creating an API Signature

Developing your application only requires access to the PayPal API sandbox. You can sign up for access to the sandbox at *http://developer.paypal.com* or *http://x.com*. Once your account is established, you can create your test accounts and obtain your API credentials. Sandbox accounts and live accounts require different processes to obtain credentials. Use the following steps for a sandbox account:

1. Go to *https://developer.paypal.com* and click "Sign Up Now."
2. Enter the requested information and click "Agree and Submit."
3. PayPal will send you an email to complete the sign-up process.
4. After confirming your email address, click "Sign Up Now" to access the sandbox.

5. Log into your sandbox account (after the initial login, this can be accessed directly by going to *https://www.sandbox.paypal.com*).

6. Click the "Test Accounts" link.

7. Click the "Create Test Account" link.

8. Choose Seller for the account type and select the other appropriate options (going with the defaults is highly recommended).

9. When using the defaults, API credentials are created automatically.

10. Click the API credentials link to access your API credentials.

 PayPal recommends you use a different login and password for your developer account than those for your live PayPal account. This will allow other people on your development team to access the sandbox and test your application without giving them access to your regular PayPal account.

For a live account, use the following steps:

1. Log into your PayPal Account. Under "My Account", click the "Profile" option.

2. Click "API Access."

3. Click "Request API Credentials."

4. Check the "Request API signature" option, and then click "Agree and Submit."

We will use the API Signature method of specifying credentials throughout this book. An API Signature is composed of three elements, as shown in Table 1-1.

Table 1-1. NVP API Signature components

API Signature component	Example value
API username	sdk-three_api1.sdk.com
API password	QFZCWN5HZM8VBG7Q
API signature	A-IzJhZZjhg29XQ2qnhapuwxIDzyAZQ92FRP5dqBzVesOkzbdUONzmOU

When you are ready to go live, you will need to activate either the Website Payments Standard or Website Payments Pro Product on your account and establish your credentials for that account. You can sign up for your account at http://www.paypal.com.

 Website Payments Pro requires additional vetting before being activated.

Creating a Name-Value Pair (NVP) Request

There are three key steps that your application must accomplish to post to the NVP API: URL encoding, constructing the request in a format the NVP API can interpret, and posting the request via HTTPS to the server.

URL encoding

Both the request to the PayPal server and the response from the server are URL encoded. This method ensures that you can transmit special characters, characters not typically allowed in a URL, and characters that have reserved meanings in a URL. For example:

```
NAME=John Doe&COMPANY= Acme Goods & Services
```

is URL encoded as follows:

```
NAME=John+Doe&Company=Acme+Goods+%26+Services
```

Each application language typically has a specific built-in URL encode method. Refer to the list in Table 1-2.

Table 1-2. URL encoding methods

Application language	Function	Method name
ASP.NET	Encode	System.Web.HttpUtility.UrlEncode(buffer, Encoding.Default)
Classic ASP	Encode	Server.URLEncode
Java	Encode	java.net.URLEncoder.encode
PHP	Encode	urlencode()
ColdFusion	Encode	URLEncodedFormatstring [, charset]

Request format

Each NVP API request is composed of required and optional parameters and their corresponding values. Parameters are not case-sensitive, but certain values such as the API Password, (PWD), are case-sensitive. The required parameters for all NVP API transactions are USER, PWD, METHOD, and VERSION. The METHOD, or type of transaction you are calling the NVP API to process, has an associated VERSION. Together the METHOD and VERSION define the exact behavior of the API operation you want performed. This will be followed by the information posted from your application, including things such as Item, Quantity, and Cost.

 API operations can change between versions, so when you change a version number, I recommend retesting your application code before going live.

Figure 1-3 outlines the API operation of an NVP request, and Figure 1-4 shows the same transaction with credentials provided.

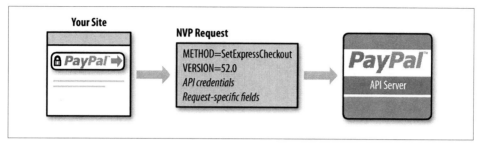

Figure 1-3. NVP request

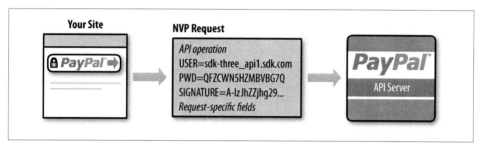

Figure 1-4. NVP request with credentials

Putting it together

Now that we have the basic elements laid out, let's put together a sample URL encoded NVP request via PHP, shown in Examples 1-1 and 1-2.

Example 1-1. developercredentials.php

```php
<?php
//PayPal NVP API Test Developer Credentials//
$paypalusername = sdk-three_api1.sdk.com;
$paypalpassword = QFZCWN5HZM8VBG7Q;
$paypalsignature = A-IzJhZZjhg29XQ2qnhapuwxIDzyAZQ92FRP5dqBzVesOkzbdUONzmOU;
$paypalserver = api-3t.sandbox.paypal.com/nvp
?>
```

Example 1-2. simpletransactionrequestprocessor.php

```php
<?php
// PayPal NVP API Simple Transaction Request Processor//
// Include the developercredentials.php file for relevant information
include("../path/outside/webroot/developercredentials.php");
// Build the credentials format of the Request String
$credentials= "USER=$paypaluser&PWD=$paypalpwd&SIGNATURE=$paypalsig";
```

```
// Designate the API Method we are calling to have handled
$method = api_method_to_use;
$version = method_version_to_use;
// Build Initial Request string
$request = $method."&".$version."&".$credentials;
// Walk the posted form elements to gather additional information
// to pass URLEncoded to API via the request string
foreach ($_POST as $key => $value){
$value = urlencode(stripslashes($value));
$request. = "&$key=$value";
};
//Build transaction and execute via curl
$ch = curl_init();
// Ensure communication is done via SSL and over a fully verified
// SSL key and certificate
curl_setopt($ch, CURLOPT_SSL_VERIFYPEER, TRUE);
curl_setopt($ch, CURLOPT_SSL_VERIFYHOST, TRUE);
// Return response as a string from server
curl_setopt($ch, CURL_RETURNTRANSFER, 1);
// Post values to server via URLEncoded string
curl_setopt($ch, CURLOPT_POST, 1);
curl_setopt($ch, CURLOPT_POSTFIELDS, $request);
//Execute Request
$response = curl_exec($ch);
?>
```

Notice that in Example 1-2, we reference the *developercredentials.php* file from a path outside the webroot. As stated earlier, this will ensure that no one can access your credentials file directly from their web browser and ensures that this information stays secure. If we were satisfied with this code and wanted to go to production, we would then change this path to the location of our production credentials file.

Parsing an NVP Response

When it comes to parsing an NVP response, your application really has to accomplish only one major step: URL decoding.

URL decoding

URL decoding the response from PayPal is basically just the reverse of URL encoding the values to pass to PayPal. For example:

```
NAME=John+Doe&Company=Acme+Goods+%26+Services
```

is decoded as follows:

```
NAME=John Doe&COMPANY= Acme Goods & Services
```

As with URL encoding, each application language typically has a URL decode method built into the language. Refer to the list in Table 1-3.

Table 1-3. URL decoding methods

Application language	Function	Method name
ASP.NET	Decode	`System.Web.HttpUtility.UrlDecode(buffer, Encoding.Default)`
Classic ASP	Decode	No built-in function; several implementation examples are available on the Internet
Java	Decode	`java.net.URLDecoder.decode`
PHP	Decode	`urldecode()`
ColdFusion	Decode	`URLDecodeurlEncodedString[, charset])`

Response format

Each NVP API response is composed of an acknowledgment (or ACK), a timestamp, a CorrelationID unique to the transaction, and a build number stating the API version used to process the transaction. This basic response is then followed by a series of name/value pairs holding the transaction data, which you can parse and handle accordingly in your application. For example, you might want to display the response information to your customer. The acknowledgment will be one of the responses outlined in Table 1-4.

Table 1-4. ACK parameter values

Type of response	Value
Successful response	`Success, SuccessWithWarning`
Partially successful response (relevant only for parallel payments; some of the payments were successful and others were not)	`PartialSuccess`
Error response code	`Failure, FailureWithWarning, Warning`

Putting it together

Now that we know how the response is formatted, we can extend the *simpletransactionrequestprocessor.php* file to handle the information returned in the `$response` string (see Example 1-3).

Example 1-3. simpletransactionrequestprocessor.php

```
//Parse $Response and handle values
$decoderesponse = explode ('&', $response);

foreach($decoderesponse as $key => $value){

    switch ($key){
        case "ACK":
        $ack = htmlspecialchars(urldecode($value));
        break;
        case "var1":
        $var1 = htmlspecialchars(urldecode($value));
        break;
```

```
        default:
        break;
        }
    }
//Your code to display or handle values returned.........
```

This is just a glimpse of what you can do with the PayPal API. The different integration methods, testing platforms, and credentials make it easy to debug and use the PayPal API to accept payments in just about any application. Next, we take a look at the simplest PayPal API method for accepting payments: Express Checkout.

CHAPTER 2

PayPal Express Checkout

Express Checkout is PayPal's premier checkout solution. It allows a customer to check out on your site, log into his PayPal account, and purchase your goods or services. Express Checkout puts PayPal in charge of data security with regard to the customer's billing and credit card information and removes that liability from the merchant. In this chapter, we will look at generic versus Express Checkout workflows, Express Checkout API operations, a simple Express Checkout integration, as well as an in-depth integration method.

Checkout Process Workflows

Let's start by looking at the process flow of a typical checkout and an Express Checkout.

Generic Checkout Workflow

Figure 2-1 shows the typical checkout flow a user experiences when buying goods or services online, which includes the following steps:

1. Customer clicks the checkout button on your shopping cart page.
2. Customer enters all shipping information.
3. Customer chooses her payment method and provides all the relevant billing and payment information.
4. Customer reviews order and pays.
5. Customer receives her order confirmation.

As you can see, this typical checkout method requires the customer to provide a lot of information at the time of purchase. This is where PayPal's Express Checkout can be a real time saver for your customers.

Figure 2-1. Generic checkout workflow

Express Checkout Workflow

Figure 2-2 shows the checkout workflow a user experiences when using PayPal's Express Checkout:

1. Customer chooses Express Checkout by clicking the "Check out with PayPal" button on your site.
2. Customer logs into PayPal.
3. Customer reviews the transaction on PayPal.
4. Customer confirms the order and pays from your site.
5. Customer receives an order confirmation.

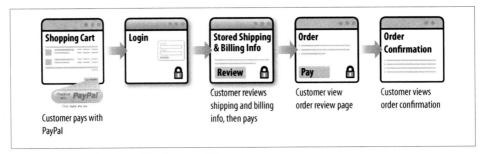

Figure 2-2. PayPal Express Checkout workflow

With Express Checkout, the customer does not need to enter his billing and shipping information each time. Consequently, customers can make purchases and move on to other tasks much more quickly.

Generic Versus Express Checkout Workflow

Table 2-1 outlines the process steps required to complete a payment during a generic checkout and Express Checkout. As you can see, Express Checkout saves both time and processing steps.

Table 2-1. Generic checkout versus Express Checkout

Checkout step	Generic checkout	Express Checkout
Select the checkout button	✓	✓
Enter shipping info	✓	-
Select payment method	✓	-
Enter payment information	✓	-
Review order	✓	✓
Confirm order	✓	✓

Express Checkout Flow

To fully implement Express Checkout, you must allow your customers two entry points into the Express Checkout payment process. Figure 2-3 outlines the complete checkout flow for Express Checkout.

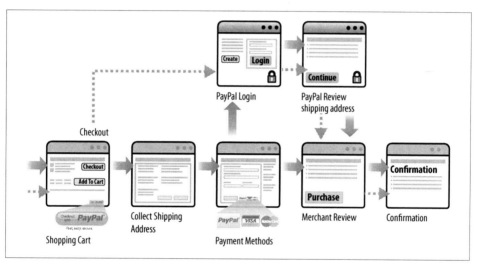

Figure 2-3. Complete Express Checkout flow

As you can see, customers can enter into the Express Checkout flow at either the Shopping Cart Checkout entry point (dotted arrow) or the Payment Methods entry point (solid arrow). Including both methods in your checkout routines is easy to implement.

Figure 2-4 outlines the Checkout Entry Point, which requires the following steps:

1. Customer clicks the "Check out with PayPal" button.
2. Customer logs into PayPal.
3. Customer confirms shipping and billing information on PayPal's site.
4. Customer is returned to your application for final review and clicks the Purchase button.
5. Customer is returned to a confirmation screen related to the purchase.

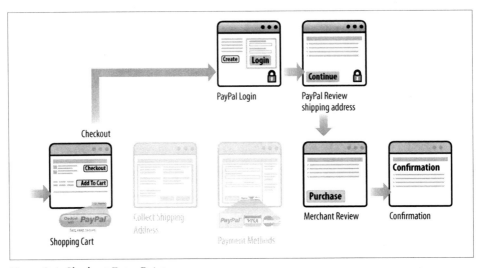

Figure 2-4. Checkout Entry Point

Figure 2-5 outlines the Payment Method Entry Point, which requires the following steps:

1. Customer clicks the checkout button on your application.
2. Customer inputs shipping information into your application.
3. Customer chooses PayPal from the list of payment methods.
4. Customer logs into PayPal.
5. Customer reviews payment information on PayPal's site.
6. Customer is returned to your application for final review and clicks the Purchase button.
7. Customer is returned to a confirmation screen related to the purchase.

A token is a value assigned by PayPal that associates the execution of API operations and commands with a specific instance of a user experience flow. Tokens are not shown in Figures 2-1 through 2-5.

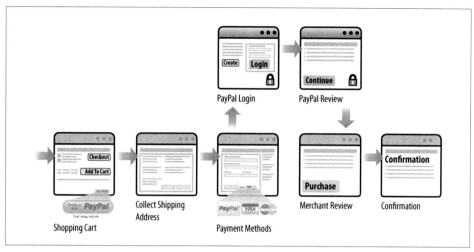

Figure 2-5. Payment Method Entry Point

PayPal Express Checkout API Operations

The PayPal NVP API provides four key methods related to Express Checkout. These operations initialize the transaction, obtain the buyer information and handle the payment, and then complete the transaction. Table 2-2 outlines these methods.

Table 2-2. Express Checkout API operations

API operation	Description
SetExpressCheckout	Sets up the Express Checkout transaction. You can specify information to customize the look and feel of the PayPal site and the information it displays. You must include the following information: • URL to the page on your website to which PayPal redirects after the buyer logs into PayPal and approves the payment successfully • URL to the page on your website to which PayPal redirects if the buyer cancels the transaction • Total amount of the order or your best estimate of the total (this should be as accurate as possible)
GetExpressCheckout Details	Obtains information about the buyer from PayPal, including shipping information.
DoExpressCheckout Payment	Completes the Express Checkout transaction, including the actual total amount of the order.
Callback	Updates the PayPal Review page with the relevant shipping options, insurance, and tax information.

Let's break down each API operation into its smaller components and outline the related request and response fields.

SetExpressCheckout

SetExpressCheckout initializes the Express Checkout session. It allows you to pass variables that format how the PayPal pages look and specify where to redirect the buyer's browser based upon success of the payment transaction.Table 2-3 outlines the fields required for SetExpressCheckout requests, and Table 2-4 outlines the field required for SetExpressCheckout responses.

Table 2-3. SetExpressCheckout request fields

Field	Description	Required?
METHOD	Must be SetExpressCheckout	Yes
RETURNURL	URL to which the customer's browser is returned after choosing to pay with PayPal. PayPal recommends that the value be the final review page on which the customer confirms the order and payment or billing agreement. Limitation: Up to 2,048 characters.	Yes
CANCELURL	URL to which the customer is returned if he does not approve the use of PayPal to pay you. PayPal recommends that the value be the original page on which the customer chose to pay with PayPal or establish a billing agreement. Limitation: Up to 2,048 characters.	Yes
PAYMENTREQUEST_*n*_AMT	The total cost of the transaction to the customer. If shipping and tax charges are known, include them in this value; if not, this value should be the current subtotal of the order. If the transaction includes one or more one-time purchases, this field must equal the sum of the purchases. Set this field to 0 if the transaction does not include a one-time purchase, for example, when you set up a billing agreement for a recurring payment that is not charged immediately. Purchase-specific fields will be ignored. Limitations: Must not exceed $10,000 USD in any currency. No currency symbol. Must have two decimal places, the decimal separator must be a period (.), and the optional thousands separator must be a comma (,).	Yes
PAYMENT_*n*_PAYMENTACTION	How you want to obtain your payment. When implementing parallel payments, this field is required and must be set to Order. • Sale indicates that this is a final sale for which you are requesting payment (this is the default). • Authorization indicates that this payment is a basic authorization subject to settlement with PayPal Authorization and Capture. • Order indicates that this payment is an order authorization subject to settlement with PayPal Authorization and Capture.	Yes

Field	Description	Required?
	If the transaction does not include a one-time purchase, this field is ignored. You cannot set this value to `Sale` in `SetExpressCheckout` request and then change this value to `Authorization` or `Order` on the final API `DoExpressCheckoutPayment` request. If the value is set to `Authorization` or `Order` in `SetExpressCheckout`, the value may be set to `Sale` or the same value (either `Authorization` or `Order`) in `DoExpressCheckoutPayment`.	
	Limitation: Up to 13 single-byte alphabetic characters.	

A complete list of all fields allowed for the `SetExpressCheckout` request method can be found in the online documentation located at *http://www.x.com/community/ppx/ documentation.*

Table 2-4. SetExpressCheckout response fields

Field	Description
TOKEN	A time-stamped token by which you identify to PayPal that you are processing this payment with Express Checkout. The token expires after three hours. If you set the token in the `SetExpressCheckout` request, the value of the token in the response is identical to the value in the request.
	Limitation: Up to 20 single-byte characters.

A complete list of all fields allowed for the `SetExpressCheckout` response method can be found in the online documentation located at *http://www.x.com/community/ppx/ documentation.*

GetExpressCheckoutDetails

`GetExpressCheckoutDetails` obtains information about an Express Checkout transaction. Only the request has required fields, as the response just echoes back the information and values enabled in `SetExpressCheckout`. Table 2-5 describes the required `GetExpressCheckoutDetails` fields.

Table 2-5. GetExpressCheckoutDetails request fields

Field	Description
METHOD	Must be `GetExpressCheckoutDetails`
TOKEN	A time-stamped token, limited to 20 single-byte characters, the value of which was returned by the `SetExpressCheckout` response

A full listing of the `GetExpressCheckoutDetails` response fields can be found in the online documentation located at *http://www.x.com/community/ppx/documentation.*

DoExpressCheckoutPayment

DoExpressCheckoutPayment completes the Express Checkout transaction and returns the payment response. If you set up a billing agreement in your SetExpressCheckout API call, the billing agreement is created when you call the DoExpressCheckoutPayment API operation. Table 2-6 lists the DoExpressCheckoutPayment request fields, and Table 2-7 describes the response fields.

Table 2-6. DoExpressCheckoutPayment request fields

Field	Description
METHOD	Must be DoExpressCheckoutPayment.
TOKEN	A time-stamped token, the value of which was returned by the SetExpressCheckout response and passed on to the GetExpressCheckoutDetails request. Limitation: Up to 20 single-byte characters.
PAYERID	Unique PayPal customer account identification number as returned by the GetExpressCheckoutDetails response. Limitation: Up to 13 single-byte alphanumeric characters.
PAYMENTREQUEST_*n*_AMT	The total cost of the transaction to the customer (required). If shipping and tax charges are known, include them in this value; if not, this value should be the current subtotal of the order. If the transaction includes one or more one-time purchases, this field must equal the sum of the purchases. Set this field to 0 if the transaction does not include a one-time purchase, for example, when you set up a billing agreement for a recurring payment that is not charged immediately. Purchase-specific fields will be ignored. Limitations: Must not exceed $10,000 USD in any currency. No currency symbol. Must have two decimal places, the decimal separator must be a period (.), and the optional thousands separator must be a comma (,).
PAYMENTREQUEST_*n*_PAYMENTACTION	How you want to obtain your payment. When implementing parallel payments, this field is required and must be set to Order. • Sale indicates that this is a final sale for which you are requesting payment (this is the default). • Authorization indicates that this payment is a basic authorization subject to settlement with PayPal Authorization and Capture. • Order indicates that this payment is an order authorization subject to settlement with PayPal Authorization and Capture. If the transaction does not include a one-time purchase, this field is ignored. You cannot set this value to Sale in SetExpressCheckout request and then change this value to Authorization or Order on the final API DoExpressCheckoutPayment request. If the value is set to

Field	Description
	Authorization or Order in SetExpressCheckout, the value may be set to Sale or the same value (either Authorization or Order) in DoExpressCheckoutPayment.
	Limitation: Up to 13 single-byte alphabetic characters.
PAYMENTREQUEST_*n*_PAYMENTREQUESTID	A unique identifier of the specific payment request, which is required for parallel payments.
	Limitation: Up to 127 single-byte character limit.

A full listing of the DoExpressCheckoutPayment request fields can be found in the online documentation located at *http://www.x.com/community/ppx/documentation*.

Table 2-7. DoExpressCheckoutPayment response fields

Field	Description
TOKEN	A time-stamped token, the value of which was returned by the SetExpressCheckout response and passed on to the GetExpressCheckoutDetails request.
	Limitation: Up to 20 single-byte characters.
PAYMENTTYPE	Information about the payment.
SUCCESSPAGEREDIRECTREQUESTED	Flag that indicates whether you need to redirect the customer to back to PayPal after completing the transaction.
PAYMENTINFO_*n*_TRANSACTIONID	Unique transaction ID of the payment. If the PaymentAction of the request was Authorization or Order, this value is your AuthorizationID for use with the Authorization and Capture APIs.
	Limitation: Up to 19 single-byte characters.
PAYMENTINFO_*n*_TRANSACTIONTYPE	The type of transaction. Valid values are cart and express-checkout.
	Limitation: Up to 15 single-byte characters.
PAYMENTINFO_*n*_PAYMENTTYPE	Indicates whether the payment is instant or delayed. Valid values are none, echeck, and instant.
	Limitation: Up to 7 single-byte characters.
PAYMENTINFO_*n*_ORDERTIME	The time/date stamp of the payment.
PAYMENTINFO_*n*_AMT	The final amount charged, including any shipping and taxes from your Merchant Profile.
	Limitations: Does not exceed $10,000 USD in any currency. No currency symbol. Regardless of currency, the decimal separator is a period (.), and the optional thousands separator is a comma (,). Equivalent to nine characters maximum for USD.
PAYMENTINFO_*n*_FEEAMT	PayPal fee amount charged for the transaction.
	Limitations: Does not exceed $10,000 USD in any currency. No currency symbol. Regardless of currency, the decimal separator is a period (.), and the optional thousands separator is a comma (,). Equivalent to nine characters maximum for USD.

Field	Description
PAYMENTINFO_*n*_TAXAMT	Tax charged on the transaction. Limitations: Does not exceed $10,000 USD in any currency. No currency symbol. Regardless of currency, the decimal separator is a period (.), and the optional thousands separator is a comma (,). Equivalent to nine characters maximum for USD.
PAYMENTINFO_*n*_EXCHANGERATE	Exchange rate if a currency conversion occurred. Relevant only if you are billing in the customer's nonprimary currency. If the customer chooses to pay with a currency other than the primary currency, the conversion occurs in the customer's account. Limitations: A decimal value that does not exceed 17 characters, including decimal points.
PAYMENTINFO_*n*_PAYMENTSTATUS	The status of the payment, which will be one of the following: • None: No status. • Canceled-Reversal: A reversal has been canceled, for example, when you win a dispute and the funds for the reversal are returned to you. • Completed: The payment has been completed and the funds have transferred successfully to your account. • Denied: You denied the payment. This will occur only if the payment was previously pending because of reasons described in the PendingReason field. • Expired: The authorization period for the payment has expired. • Failed: The payment failed. This occurs only when the payment was made from your customer's bank draft account. • In-Progress: Transaction has not terminated, most likely due to an authorization awaiting completion. • Partially-Refunded: Payment has been partially refunded. • Pending: Payment is still pending for reasons described in the PendingReason field. • Refunded: You refunded the payment. • Reversed: Payment was reversed due to a charge back or other reversal. The funds have been removed from your account balance and returned to the buyer. The reason will be described in the ReasonCode field. • Processed: Payment has been accepted. • Voided: Authorization for the transaction has been voided.
PAYMENTINFO_*n*_PROTECTION ELIGIBILITY	The type of seller protection in force for the transaction, which is one of the following values: • Eligible: Seller is protected by PayPal's Seller protection policy for Unauthorized Payments and Item Not Received. • PartiallyEligible: Seller is protected by PayPal's Seller Protection Policy for Item Not Received.

Field	Description
	• Ineligible: Seller is not protected under the Seller Protection Policy.
PAYMENTREQUEST_*n*_PAYMENTREQUESTID	The unique identifier of the specific payment request. The value should match the one passed in the DoExpressCheckout request. Limitation: Up to 127 single-byte characters.
L_PAYMENTINFO_*n*_FMFfilterIDn	Filter ID, including the filter type (PENDING, REPORT, or DENY), the filter ID, and the entry number, *n*, starting from 0. Filter ID is one of the following values:
	• 1 = AVS No Match
	• 2 = AVS Partial Match
	• 3 = AVS Unavailable/Unsupported
	• 4 = Card Security Code (CSC) Mismatch
	• 5 = Maximum Transaction Amount
	• 6 = Unconfirmed Address
	• 7 = Country Monitor
	• 8 = Large Order Number
	• 9 = Billing/Shipping Address Mismatch
	• 10 = Risky Zip Code
	• 11 = Suspected Freight Forwarder Check
	• 12 = Total Purchase Price Minimum
	• 13 = IP Address Velocity
	• 14 = Risky Email Address Domain Check
	• 15 = Risky Bank Identification Number (BIN) Check
	• 16 = Risky IP Address Range
	• 17 = PayPal Fraud Model
L_PAYMENTINFO_*n*_FMFfilterNAME*n*	Filter name, including the filter type (PENDING, REPORT, or DENY), the filter NAME, and the entry number, *n*, starting from 0.
PAYMENTREQUEST_*n*_SHORTMESSAGE	Payment error short message.
PAYMEMNTREQUEST_*n*_LONGMESSAGE	Payment error long message.
PAYMENTREQUEST_*n*_ERRORCODE	Payment error code.
PAYMENTREQUEST_*n*_SEVERITYCODE	Payment error severity code.
PAYMENTREQUEST_*n*_ACK	Application-specific error values indicating more about the error condition.
SHIPPINGCALCULATIONMODE	Describes how the options that were presented to the user were determined, and is one of the following values:
	• API - Callback
	• API - Flatrate
INSURANCEOPTIONSELECTED	The Yes/No option that you chose for insurance.

Field	Description
SHIPPINGOPTIONISDEFAULT	Is true if the buyer chose the default shipping option. Value will be either TRUE or FALSE.
SHIPPINGOPTIONAMOUNT	The shipping amount that was chosen by the buyer. Limitations: Must not exceed $10,000 USD in any currency. No currency symbol. Must have two decimal places, the decimal separator must be a period (.), and the optional thousands separator must be a comma (,).
SHIPPINGOPTIONNAME	This is true if the buyer chose the default shipping option.
PAYMENTREQUEST_n_SELLERPAYPAL ACCOUNTID	Unique identifier for the merchant. For parallel payments, this field contains either the Payer ID or the email address of the merchant.

Callback

Callback allows you to return any relevant shipping information to the PayPal review page. Table 2-8 outlines the required Fields for Callback requests and Table 2-9 outlines the required fields for Callback responses.

Table 2-8. Callback request fields

Field	Description
METHOD	Must be Callback (required).
CURRENCYCODE	The three-character currency code for the transaction from the Express Checkout API (required). Default is USD.
L_NAMEn	Item name from the Express Checkout API. Parameters must be numbered sequentially starting with 0 (e.g., L_NAME0, L_NAME1).
L_NUMBERn	Item number from the Express Checkout API. Parameters must be numbered sequentially starting with 0 (e.g., L_NUMBER0, L_NUMBER1).
L_DESCn	Item description from the Express Checkout API. Parameters must be numbered sequentially starting with 0 (e.g., L_DESC0, L_DESC1).
L_AMTn	Item unit price from the Express Checkout API. Parameters must be numbered sequentially starting with 0 (e.g., L_AMT0, L_AMT1).
L_QTYn	Item unit quantity from the Express Checkout API. Parameters must be numbered sequentially starting with 0 (e.g., L_QTY0, L_QTY1).
L_ITEMWEIGHTVALUEn L_ITEMWEIGHTUNITn	The weight of the item. You can pass this data to the shipping carrier as is, with no additional database query. Parameters must be numbered sequentially starting with 0 (e.g., L_ITEM WEIGHTVALUE0, L_ITEMWEIGHTVALUE1).
L_ITEMHEIGHTVALUEn L_ITEMHEIGHTUNITn	The height of the item. You can pass this data to the shipping carrier as is, with no additional database query. Parameters must be numbered sequentially starting with 0 (e.g., L_ITEM HEIGHTVALUE0, L_ITEMHEIGHTVALUE1).
L_ITEMWIDTHVALUEn L_ITEMWIDTHUNITn	The width of the item. You can pass this data to the shipping carrier as is, with no additional database query. Parameters must be numbered sequentially starting with 0 (e.g., L_ITEM WIDTHVALUE0, L_ITEMWIDTHVALUE1).

Field	Description
L_ITEMLENGTHVALUE*n* L_ITEMLENGTHUNIT*n*	The length of the item. You can pass this data to the shipping carrier as is, with no additional database query. Parameters must be numbered sequentially starting with 0 (e.g., L_ITEM LENGTHVALUE0, L_ITEMLENGTHVALUE1).
SHIPTOSTREET	The first street address. This is required if using a shipping address. Limitation: Up to 100 single-byte characters.
SHIPTOSTREET2	The second street address. Limitation: Up to 100 single-byte characters.
SHIPTOCITY	The name of the city. This is required if using a shipping address. Limitation: Up to 40 single-byte characters.
SHIPTOSTATE	The state or province. Required if using a shipping address. Limitation: Up to 40 single-byte characters.
SHIPTOZIP	U.S. postal zip code or other country-specific postal code. Required if using a U.S. shipping address; may be required for other countries. Limitation: Up to 20 single-byte characters.
SHIPTOCOUNTRY	Country code. Required if using a shipping address. Limitation: Up to two single-byte characters.

A complete list of all fields allowed for the Callback request method and response method can be found in the online documentation at *http://www.x.com/community/ ppx/documentation*.

Table 2-9. Callback response fields

Field	Description
METHOD	Must be CallbackResponse (required).
CURRENCYCODE	The three-character currency code for the transaction from the Express Checkout API (required).
L_SHIPPINGOPTIONNAME*n*	The internal/system name of a shipping option (e.g., Air, Ground, Expedited). This field is required. Parameters must be ordered sequentially starting with 0 (e.g., L_SHIPPINGOPTIONNAME0, L_SHIPPINGOPTIONNAME1). Limitation: Up to 50 characters.
L_SHIPPINGOPTIONLABEL*n*	The label for the shipping options displayed to the buyer (e.g., Air: Next Day, Expedited: 3-5 days, Ground: 5-7 days). This field is required. Labels can be localized based on the buyer's locale. Parameters must be numbered sequentially starting with 0 (e.g., L_SHIPPINGOPTIONLABEL0, L_SHIPPINGOPTIONLABEL1). Limitation: Up to 50 characters.
L_SHIPPINGOPTIONAMOUNT*n*	Amount of the shipping option. Parameters must be numbered sequentially starting with 0 (e.g., L_SHIPPINGOPTIONAMOUNT0, L_SHIPPINGOPTIONAMOUNT1). Limitations: Must not exceed $10,000 USD in any currency. No currency symbol allowed. The decimal separator must be a period (.), regardless of currency, and the optional thousands separator must be a comma(,). Equivalent to nine characters maximum for USD.
L_SHIPPINGOPTIONISDEFAULT	The default option selected for the buyer; this is also reflected in the "default" total (required).

Simple Express Checkout Integration

The simplest Express Checkout integration requires execution of only two PayPal API operations: SetExpressCheckout and DoExpressCheckoutPayment. For example, optionally, you can call GetExpressCheckoutDetails to error check the information provided to SetExpressCheckout against the form values and provide the customer a Confirm Transaction screen before finalizing the payment.

Setting Up the Transaction

To set up an Express Checkout transaction, you must first invoke the SetExpressCheckout API to provide sufficient information to initiate the payment flow and redirect your customer to PayPal if the operation is successful.

When you initiate the Express Checkout transaction, you specify values in the SetExpressCheckout request, and then call the API. The values you specify control the PayPal page flow and options available to your customers.

Let's look at setting up a simple Express Checkout transaction.

1. First we need to specify the total dollar amount of the transaction, if known; otherwise, specify the subtotal. Refer to Table 2-3's PAYMENTREQUEST_*n*_AMT field description for requirements and restrictions.

   AMT=*amount*

   CURRENCYCODE=*currencyID*

2. Specify the return URL. This is the page on your site that you want PayPal to redirect the customer to after the customer logs into PayPal and approves the payment. Typically, the customer is redirected to a secure page on your site via SSL (*https://*).

   RETURNURL=*return_url*

3. Specify the cancel URL. This is the page on your site you want PayPal to redirect the customer to if the buyer does not approve the payment. Typically, the customer is redirected to a secure page on your site via SSL (*https://*).

   CANCELURL=*cancel_url*

4. Specify the payment action. Even though the action is a Sale, it is best to explicitly set the payment action. Refer to Table 2-3's PAYMENT_*n*_PAYMENTACTION field description for allowed values.

5. Execute the SetExpressCheckoutAPI operation and test that the response was successful. To test for success, check to see whether the API returns a TOKEN and other variables.

You can piggyback parameters between pages on your site in the return URL call as well as the cancel URL call. For example, you can set your return URL to specify additional parameters using something like *https://your.domain.ext/returnpage.php?param1=val1&param2=val2*, etc. This allows you to pass parameters from the transaction without making a `GetExpressCheckoutDetails` API call, or pass custom parameters not provided by the `SetExpressCheckout` API.

To execute the transaction, you must invoke the `DoExpressCheckoutPayment` operation. This is accomplished through the following steps:

1. Specify the TOKEN value returned by PayPal when it redirects the buyer's browser to your site.

   `TOKEN=tokenValue`

2. Specify the payer ID returned by PayPal when it redirects the customer's browser to your site.

   `PAYERID=id`

3. Specify the total amount of the payment, including shipping, handling, and tax, and include the currency if not in U.S. dollars.

   `AMT=amount`

   `CURRENCYCODE=currencyID`

4. Specify the payment action. Even though the action is a `Sale`, it is best to explicitly set the payment action. Refer to Table 2-3's `PAYMENT_n_PAYMENTACTION` field description for allowed values.

5. Execute the `DoExpressCheckoutAPI` operation, and test that the response was successful.

Express Checkout Integration

PayPal Express Checkout is the quickest and best solution for straight-out shopping cart checkouts. PayPal's Integration Wizard, found at *https://www.paypal-labs.com/integrationwizard/ecpaypal/main.php*, helps you implement Express Checkout on your site. The wizard takes you through five configuration steps, described next.

The Integration Wizard starts by presenting a basic overview of what the tool will do. You can choose to watch the introduction or skip it at this point (Figure 2-6).

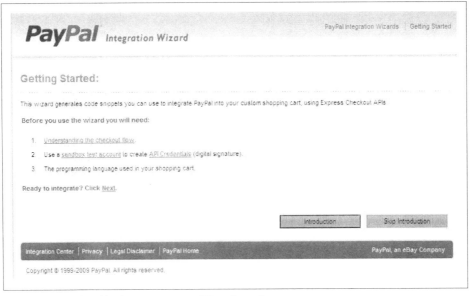

Figure 2-6. Express Checkout Integration Wizard opening screen

Step 1 allows you to choose the programming language you want to use for the integration (see Figure 2-7). For the purposes of this example we are going to use PHP, but you can choose any of the following options:

- Active Server Pages (ASP)
- ASP.NET-C#(ASPX)
- ASP.NET-VB.NET(ASPX)
- Java Server Pages (JSP)
- Java SDK
- PHP

You also are asked to specify the return and cancel URLs. The return URL is where the purchaser will be returned to once the transaction is completed. The cancel URL is where the purchaser is sent to if she cancels the checkout, typically back to your site's shopping cart. The payment type will be one of the following:

- Sale
- Authorization
- Order

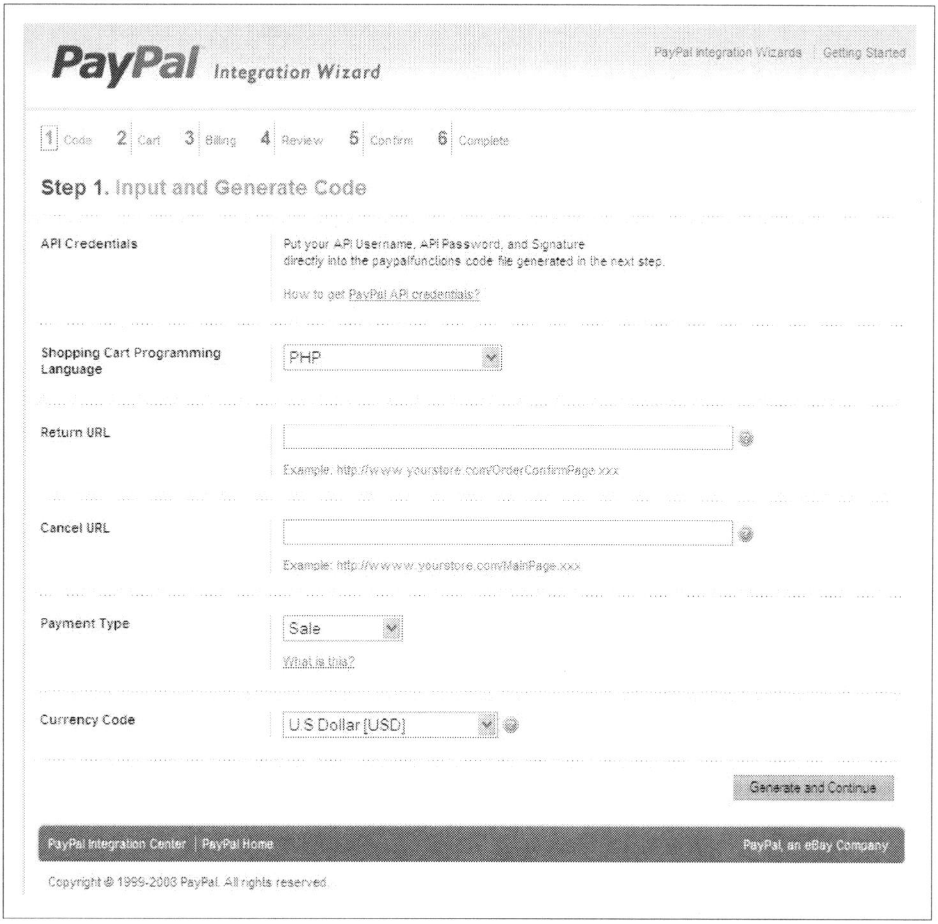

Figure 2-7. Express Checkout Integration Wizard step 1

The Currency Code section contains a list of currencies, both foreign and domestic, from which to choose. For this example, we will choose U.S. Dollar [USD].

The form element generated in step 2 (see Figure 2-8) wraps around your shopping cart order form, and allows you to submit the payment via PayPal (see Example 2-6). It will also generate a button on-screen. You must be sure to enable a PHP $_SESSION and set the variable $_SESSION['Payment_Amount'] that contains the amount of the purchase; otherwise, the generated code will not work properly.

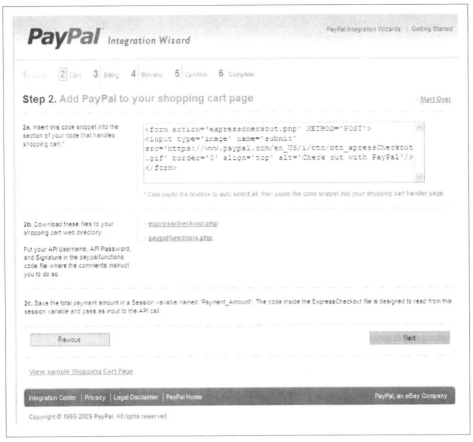

Figure 2-8. Express Checkout Integration Wizard step 2

You now have the option to download *expresscheckout.php* (see Example 2-1), and *paypalfunctions.php* (see Example 2-2). You will need to modify the *paypalfunction.php* file with your API credentials. For instructions on creating those credentials, refer to "Creating an API Signature" on page 4. Additionally, after you have completed testing and are ready to go live, change $SandboxFlag='true' to $SandboxFlag= 'false'. This will change the endpoints to the live PayPal endpoint.

> For security reasons, I recommend putting your *paypalfunctions.php* file in a location accessible to *expresscheckout.php* and the other generated files, but outside your main webroot. This will help to prevent anyone from potentially obtaining your API credentials.

Step 3 generates code for your billing page that will be used if someone chooses PayPal from the billing options page instead of the main shopping cart page (see Figure 2-9).

Figure 2-9. Express Checkout Integration Wizard step 3

You must be sure to enable a PHP $_SESSION and set the variable $_SESSION['*Pay ment_Amount*']that contains the amount of the purchase; otherwise, the generated code will not work properly. You can copy the code from the box generated by the Wizard, and paste it into your billing handler (see Example 2-3).

Step 4 (Figure 2-10) generates code to add to your shipping page. You can copy the code from the box generated by the Wizard and paste it into your shipping handler (see Example 2-4). Step 5 (Figure 2-11) generates code for your order confirmation page. You can copy the code from the box generated by the Wizard and paste it into your order confirmation handler (see Example 2-5). Step 6 completes the Integration Wizard, as shown in Figure 2-12.

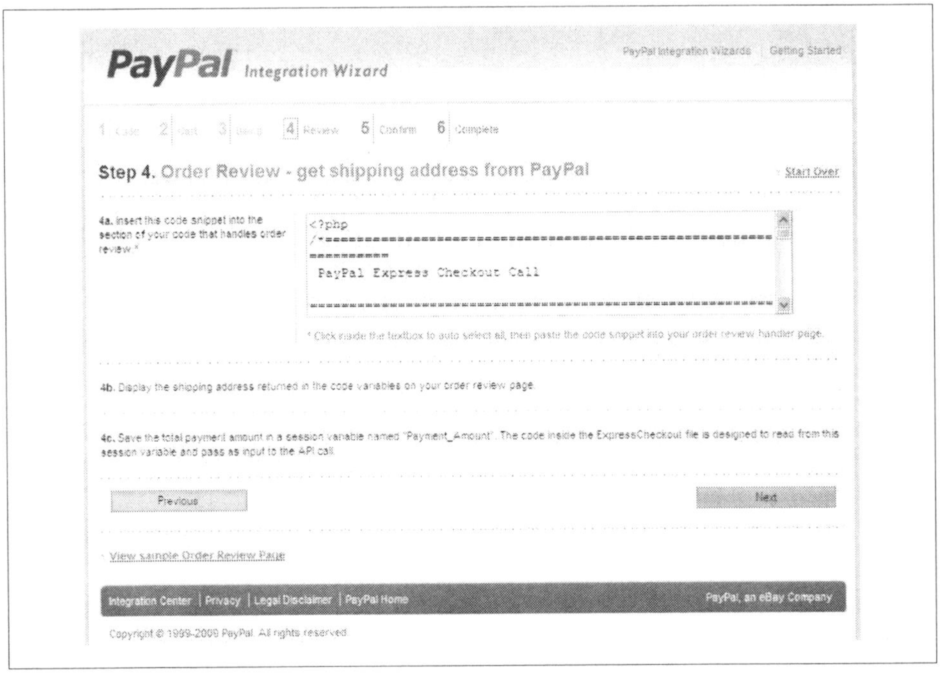

Figure 2-10. *Express Checkout Integration Wizard step 4*

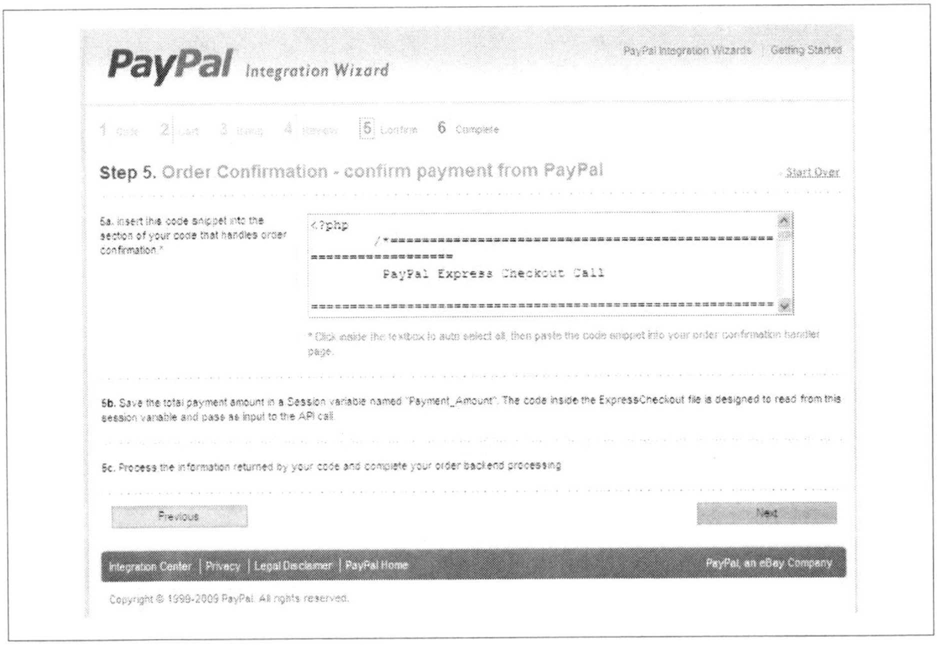

Figure 2-11. *Express Checkout Integration Wizard step 5*

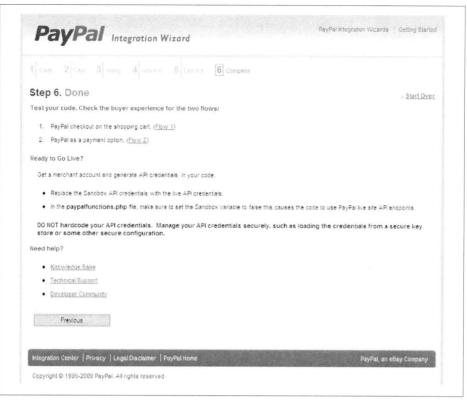

Figure 2-12. Express Checkout Integration Wizard step 6

Example 2-1. paypalfunctions.php

```php
<?php
/*******************************************
PayPal API Module

Defines all the global variables and the wrapper functions
*******************************************/
$PROXY_HOST = '127.0.0.1';
$PROXY_PORT = '808';

$SandboxFlag = true;

//'-----------------------------------
//' PayPal API Credentials
//' Replace <API_USERNAME> with your API Username
//' Replace <API_PASSWORD> with your API Password
//' Replace <API_SIGNATURE> with your Signature
//'-----------------------------------
$API_UserName="mdbald_1287976381_biz_api1.michaelbalderas.com";
$API_Password="1287976406";
$API_Signature="APOxIKm-FxOtSYmLLbuPFN42APwdAhhNTtvJ8YhTD2ALC9poKmbhBaf6";
```

```
// BN Code is only applicable for partners
$sBNCode = "PP-ECWizard";


/*
' Define the PayPal Redirect URLs.
' This is the URL where the buyer is first sent to authorize payment with their
' PayPal account. Change the URL depending on whether you are testing on the sandbox
' or the live PayPal site.
'
' For the sandbox, the URL is
' https://www.sandbox.paypal.com/webscr&cmd=_express-checkout&token=
' For the live site, the URL is
' https://www.paypal.com/webscr&cmd=_express-checkout&token=
*/

if ($SandboxFlag == true)
{
 $API_Endpoint = "https://api-3t.sandbox.paypal.com/nvp";
 $PAYPAL_URL = "https://www.sandbox.paypal.com/webscr?cmd=_express-checkout&token=";
}
else
{
 $API_Endpoint = "https://api-3t.paypal.com/nvp";
 $PAYPAL_URL = "https://www.paypal.com/cgi-bin/webscr?cmd=_express-checkout&token=";
}

$USE_PROXY = false;
$version="64";

if (session_id() == "")
 session_start();

/* An express checkout transaction starts with a token that identifies
    to PayPal your transaction. In this example, when the script sees
    a token, the script knows that the buyer has already authorized
    payment through PayPal.  If no token was found, the action is
    to send the buyer to PayPal to first authorize payment.
    */

/*
'-------------------------------------------------------------------------------
' Purpose: Prepares the parameters for the SetExpressCheckout API Call.
' Inputs:
'   paymentAmount:  Total value of the shopping cart
'   currencyCodeType: Currency code value the PayPal API
'   paymentType:    paymentType has to be one of the following values:
'                   Sale or Order or Authorization
'   returnURL:      The page where buyers return to after they are done
'                   with the payment review on PayPal
'   cancelURL:      The page where buyers return to when they cancel the
'                   payment review on PayPal
'-------------------------------------------------------------------------------
*/
```

```
function CallShortcutExpressCheckout( $paymentAmount, $currencyCodeType,
        $paymentType, $returnURL, $cancelURL)
{
 //---------------------------------------------------------------------------
 // Construct the parameter string that describes the SetExpressCheckout
 // API call in the shortcut implementation

 $nvpstr="&PAYMENTREQUEST_0_AMT=". $paymentAmount;
 $nvpstr = $nvpstr . "&PAYMENTREQUEST_0_PAYMENTACTION=" . $paymentType;
 $nvpstr = $nvpstr . "&RETURNURL=" . $returnURL;
 $nvpstr = $nvpstr . "&CANCELURL=" . $cancelURL;
 $nvpstr = $nvpstr . "&PAYMENTREQUEST_0_CURRENCYCODE=" . $currencyCodeType;

 $_SESSION["currencyCodeType"] = $currencyCodeType;
 $_SESSION["PaymentType"] = $paymentType;

 //'--------------------------------------------------------------------------
 //' Make the API call to PayPal
 //' If the API call succeeded, then redirect the buyer to PayPal to begin to
 //' authorize payment.
 //' If an error occurred, show the resulting errors.
 //'--------------------------------------------------------------------------
    $resArray=hash_call("SetExpressCheckout", $nvpstr);
 $ack = strtoupper($resArray["ACK"]);
 if($ack=="SUCCESS" || $ack=="SUCCESSWITHWARNING")
 {
  $token = urldecode($resArray["TOKEN"]);
  $_SESSION['TOKEN']=$token;
 }

    return $resArray;
}

/*
'--------------------------------------------------------------------------
' Purpose: Prepares the parameters for the SetExpressCheckout API Call.
' Inputs:
'   paymentAmount:  Total value of the shopping cart
'   currencyCodeType: Currency code value the PayPal API
'   paymentType: paymentType has to be one of the following values: Sale or Order or
'                Authorization
'   returnURL:    The page where buyers return to after they are done with the payment
'                review on PayPal
'   cancelURL:    The page where buyers return to when they cancel the payment review
'                on PayPal
'   shipToName:   The Ship to Name entered on the merchant's site
'   shipToStreet: The Ship to Street entered on the merchant's site
'   shipToCity:   the Ship to City entered on the merchant's site
'   shipToState:  The Ship to State entered on the merchant's site
'   shipToCountryCode: The Code for Ship to Country entered on the merchant's site
'   shipToZip:    The Ship to ZipCode entered on the merchant's site
'   shipToStreet2: The Ship to Street2 entered on the merchant's site
'   phoneNum:     The phoneNum  entered on the merchant's site
'--------------------------------------------------------------------------
*/
```

```
function CallMarkExpressCheckout( $paymentAmount, $currencyCodeType, $paymentType,
        $returnURL, $cancelURL, $shipToName, $shipToStreet, $shipToCity,
        $shipToState, $shipToCountryCode, $shipToZip, $shipToStreet2, $phoneNum
        )
{
//-------------------------------------------------------------------------------
// Construct the parameter string that describes the SetExpressCheckout API call in
// the shortcut implementation

$nvpstr="&PAYMENTREQUEST_0_AMT=". $paymentAmount;
$nvpstr = $nvpstr . "&PAYMENTREQUEST_0_PAYMENTACTION=" . $paymentType;
$nvpstr = $nvpstr . "&RETURNURL=" . $returnURL;
$nvpstr = $nvpstr . "&CANCELURL=" . $cancelURL;
$nvpstr = $nvpstr . "&PAYMENTREQUEST_0_CURRENCYCODE=" . $currencyCodeType;
$nvpstr = $nvpstr . "&ADDROVERRIDE=1";
$nvpstr = $nvpstr . "&PAYMENTREQUEST_0_SHIPTONAME=" . $shipToName;
$nvpstr = $nvpstr . "&PAYMENTREQUEST_0_SHIPTOSTREET=" . $shipToStreet;
$nvpstr = $nvpstr . "&PAYMENTREQUEST_0_SHIPTOSTREET2=" . $shipToStreet2;
$nvpstr = $nvpstr . "&PAYMENTREQUEST_0_SHIPTOCITY=" . $shipToCity;
$nvpstr = $nvpstr . "&PAYMENTREQUEST_0_SHIPTOSTATE=" . $shipToState;
$nvpstr = $nvpstr . "&PAYMENTREQUEST_0_SHIPTOCOUNTRYCODE=" . $shipToCountryCode;
$nvpstr = $nvpstr . "&PAYMENTREQUEST_0_SHIPTOZIP=" . $shipToZip;
$nvpstr = $nvpstr . "&PAYMENTREQUEST_0_SHIPTOPHONENUM=" . $phoneNum;

$_SESSION["currencyCodeType"] = $currencyCodeType;
$_SESSION["PaymentType"] = $paymentType;

//'------------------------------------------------------------------------------
//' Make the API call to PayPal
//' If the API call succeeded, then redirect the buyer to PayPal to begin to
//' authorize payment.
//' If an error occurred, show the resulting errors.
//'------------------------------------------------------------------------------
  $resArray=hash_call("SetExpressCheckout", $nvpstr);
$ack = strtoupper($resArray["ACK"]);
if($ack=="SUCCESS" || $ack=="SUCCESSWITHWARNING")
{
 $token = urldecode($resArray["TOKEN"]);
 $_SESSION['TOKEN']=$token;
}

  return $resArray;
}

/*
'------------------------------------------------------------------------------
' Purpose: Prepares the parameters for the GetExpressCheckoutDetails API Call.
'
' Inputs:
'  None
' Returns:
'  The NVP Collection object of the GetExpressCheckoutDetails Call Response.
'------------------------------------------------------------------------------
*/
function GetShippingDetails( $token )
```

```
{
  //'---------------------------------------------------------------
  //' At this point, the buyer has finished authorizing the payment
  //' on PayPal.  The function will call PayPal to obtain the details
  //' of the authorization, including any of the buyer's shipping information.
  //' Remember, the authorization is not a completed transaction
  //' at this stage - the buyer still needs an additional step to finalize
  //' the transaction.
  //'---------------------------------------------------------------

    //'--------------------------------------------------------------------------
  //'   Build a second API request to PayPal, using the token as the
  //'   ID to get the details on the payment authorization
  //'--------------------------------------------------------------------------
    $nvpstr="&TOKEN=" . $token;

  //'--------------------------------------------------------------------------
  //' Make the API call and store the results in an array.
  //' If the call was a success, show the authorization details, and provide
  //' an action to complete the payment.
  //' If failed, show the error.
  //'--------------------------------------------------------------------------
    $resArray=hash_call("GetExpressCheckoutDetails",$nvpstr);
    $ack = strtoupper($resArray["ACK"]);
if($ack == "SUCCESS" || $ack=="SUCCESSWITHWARNING")
 {
  $_SESSION['payer_id'] = $resArray['PAYERID'];
 }
 return $resArray;
}

/*
'--------------------------------------------------------------------------------------
' Purpose: Prepares the parameters for the GetExpressCheckoutDetails API Call.
'
' Inputs:
'   sBNCode: The BN code used by PayPal to track the transactions
'   from a given shopping cart.
' Returns:
'   The NVP Collection object of the GetExpressCheckoutDetails Call Response.
'--------------------------------------------------------------------------------------
*/
function ConfirmPayment( $FinalPaymentAmt )
{
 /* Gather the information to make the final call to
    finalize the PayPal payment. The variable nvpstr
    holds the name-value pairs.
    */


//Format the other parameters that were stored in the session from the previous calls
$token = urlencode($_SESSION['TOKEN']);
$paymentType = urlencode($_SESSION['PaymentType']);
$currencyCodeType = urlencode($_SESSION['currencyCodeType']);
$payerID = urlencode($_SESSION['payer_id']);
```

```
$serverName = urlencode($_SERVER['SERVER_NAME']);

$nvpstr  = '&TOKEN=' . $token . '&PAYERID=' . $payerID .
           '&PAYMENTREQUEST_0_PAYMENTACTION='.
           $paymentType . '&PAYMENTREQUEST_0_AMT=' . $FinalPaymentAmt .
           '&PAYMENTREQUEST_0_CURRENCYCODE=' . $currencyCodeType .'&IPADDRESS='.
           $serverName;

 /* Make the call to PayPal to finalize payment
    If an error occurred, show the resulting errors.
    */
$resArray=hash_call("DoExpressCheckoutPayment",$nvpstr);

 /* Display the API response back to the browser.
    If the response from PayPal was a success, display the response parameters.
    If the response was an error, display the errors received using APIError.php.
    */
$ack = strtoupper($resArray["ACK"]);

 return $resArray;
}

/*
'--------------------------------------------------------------------------------
'
' Purpose: This function makes a DoDirectPayment API call
'
' Inputs:
'  paymentType:   paymentType has to be one of the following values: Sale or Order or
'                 Authorization
'  paymentAmount:  Total value of the shopping cart
'  currencyCode: Currency code value in the PayPal API
'  firstName: first name as it appears on credit card
'  lastName: Last name as it appears on credit card
'  street: Buyer's street address line as it appears on credit card
'  city: Buyer's city
'  state: Buyer's state
'  countryCode: Buyer's country code
'  zip: Buyer's zip
'  creditCardType: Buyer's credit card type (e.g., Visa, MasterCard ... )
'  creditCardNumber: Buyer's credit card number without any spaces, dashes, or any other
'                 characters
'  expDate: Credit card expiration date
'  cvv2: Card Verification Value
'
'--------------------------------------------------------------------------------
'
' Returns:
'  The NVP Collection object of the DoDirectPayment Call Response.
'--------------------------------------------------------------------------------
*/
```

```php
function DirectPayment( $paymentType, $paymentAmount, $creditCardType, $creditCardNumber,
    $expDate, $cvv2, $firstName, $lastName, $street, $city, $state, $zip,
    $countryCode, $currencyCode )
{
 //Construct the parameter string that describes DoDirectPayment
 $nvpstr = "&AMT=" . $paymentAmount;
 $nvpstr = $nvpstr . "&CURRENCYCODE=" . $currencyCode;
 $nvpstr = $nvpstr . "&PAYMENTACTION=" . $paymentType;
 $nvpstr = $nvpstr . "&CREDITCARDTYPE=" . $creditCardType;
 $nvpstr = $nvpstr . "&ACCT=" . $creditCardNumber;
 $nvpstr = $nvpstr . "&EXPDATE=" . $expDate;
 $nvpstr = $nvpstr . "&CVV2=" . $cvv2;
 $nvpstr = $nvpstr . "&FIRSTNAME=" . $firstName;
 $nvpstr = $nvpstr . "&LASTNAME=" . $lastName;
 $nvpstr = $nvpstr . "&STREET=" . $street;
 $nvpstr = $nvpstr . "&CITY=" . $city;
 $nvpstr = $nvpstr . "&STATE=" . $state;
 $nvpstr = $nvpstr . "&COUNTRYCODE=" . $countryCode;
 $nvpstr = $nvpstr . "&IPADDRESS=" . $_SERVER['REMOTE_ADDR'];

 $resArray=hash_call("DoDirectPayment", $nvpstr);

 return $resArray;
}


/**
  '-----------------------------------------------------------------------------
  * hash_call: Function to perform the API call to PayPal using API signature
  * @methodName is name of API  method.
  * @nvpStr is nvp string.
  * Returns an associative array containing the response from the server.
  '-----------------------------------------------------------------------------
*/
function hash_call($methodName,$nvpStr)
{
 //declaring of global variables
 global $API_Endpoint, $version, $API_UserName, $API_Password, $API_Signature;
 global $USE_PROXY, $PROXY_HOST, $PROXY_PORT;
 global $gv_ApiErrorURL;
 global $sBNCode;

 //setting the curl parameters.
 $ch = curl_init();
 curl_setopt($ch, CURLOPT_URL,$API_Endpoint);
 curl_setopt($ch, CURLOPT_VERBOSE, 1);

 //turning off the server and peer verification(TrustManager Concept).
 curl_setopt($ch, CURLOPT_SSL_VERIFYPEER, FALSE);
 curl_setopt($ch, CURLOPT_SSL_VERIFYHOST, FALSE);

 curl_setopt($ch, CURLOPT_RETURNTRANSFER,1);
 curl_setopt($ch, CURLOPT_POST, 1);
```

```php
//if USE_PROXY constant set to TRUE in Constants.php, then only proxy will be enabled.
//Set proxy name to PROXY_HOST and port number to PROXY_PORT in constants.php
if($USE_PROXY)
 curl_setopt ($ch, CURLOPT_PROXY, $PROXY_HOST. ":" . $PROXY_PORT);

//NVPRequest for submitting to server
$nvpreq = "METHOD=" . urlencode($methodName) . "&VERSION=" . urlencode($version) .
       "&PWD=".
       urlencode($API_Password) . "&USER=" . urlencode($API_UserName) . "&SIGNATURE=".
       urlencode($API_Signature) . $nvpStr . "&BUTTONSOURCE=" . urlencode($sBNCode);

//setting the nvpreq as POST FIELD to curl
curl_setopt($ch, CURLOPT_POSTFIELDS, $nvpreq);

//getting response from server
$response = curl_exec($ch);

//converting NVPResponse to an Associative Array
$nvpResArray=deformatNVP($response);
$nvpReqArray=deformatNVP($nvpreq);
$_SESSION['nvpReqArray']=$nvpReqArray;

if (curl_errno($ch))
{
 // moving to display page to display curl errors
   $_SESSION['curl_error_no']=curl_errno($ch) ;
   $_SESSION['curl_error_msg']=curl_error($ch);

   //Execute the error-handling module to display errors.
}
else
{
  //closing the curl
   curl_close($ch);
}

 return $nvpResArray;
}

/*'-----------------------------------------------------------------------------
 Purpose: Redirects to PayPal.com site.
 Inputs:  NVP string.
 Returns:
 -----------------------------------------------------------------------------
*/
function RedirectToPayPal ( $token )
{
 global $PAYPAL_URL;

 // Redirect to paypal.com here
 $payPalURL = $PAYPAL_URL . $token;
 header("Location: ".$payPalURL);
}
```

```
/*'------------------------------------------------------------------------
 * This function will take NVPString and convert it to an Associative Array and
 * then will decode the response.
 * It is useful to search for a particular key and display the arrays.
 * @nvpstr is NVPString.
 * @nvpArray is Associative Array.
 ------------------------------------------------------------------------
 */
function deformatNVP($nvpstr)
{
 $intial=0;
 $nvpArray = array();

 while(strlen($nvpstr))
 {
 //position of Key
 $keypos= strpos($nvpstr,'=');
 //position of value
 $valuepos = strpos($nvpstr,'&') ? strpos($nvpstr,'&'): strlen($nvpstr);

 /*getting the Key and Value values and storing in a Associative Array*/
 $keyval=substr($nvpstr,$intial,$keypos);
 $valval=substr($nvpstr,$keypos+1,$valuepos-$keypos-1);
 //decoding the respose
 $nvpArray[urldecode($keyval)] =urldecode( $valval);
 $nvpstr=substr($nvpstr,$valuepos+1,strlen($nvpstr));
     }
 return $nvpArray;
}

?>
```

Example 2-2. expresscheckout.php

```php
<?php

require_once ("paypalfunctions.php");
// ===================================
// PayPal Express Checkout Module
// ===================================

//'-----------------------------------
//' The paymentAmount is the total value of
//' the shopping cart, which was set
//' earlier in a session variable
//' by the shopping cart page.
//'-----------------------------------
$paymentAmount = $_SESSION["Payment_Amount"];

//'-----------------------------------
//' The currencyCodeType and paymentType
//' are set to the selections made in the Integration Assistant.
//'-----------------------------------
$currencyCodeType = "USD";
$paymentType = "Sale";
```

```
//'-----------------------------------
//' The returnURL is the location where buyers return to when a
//' payment has been succesfully authorized.
//'
//' This is set to the value entered in the Integration Assistant.
//'-----------------------------------
$returnURL = "http://www.michaelbalderas.com/paypal/expresscheckout/OrderConfirm.php";


//'-----------------------------------
//' The cancelURL is the location buyers are sent to when they hit the
//' cancel button during authorization of payment during the PayPal flow.
//'
//' This is set to the value entered in the Integration Assistant.
//'-----------------------------------
$cancelURL = "http://www.michaelbalderas.com/paypal/expresscheckout/shoppingcart.php";


//'-----------------------------------
//' Calls the SetExpressCheckout API call
//'
//' The CallShortcutExpressCheckout function is defined in the file PayPalFunctions.php,
//' which is included at the top of this file.
//'----------------------------------------------------
$resArray = CallShortcutExpressCheckout ($paymentAmount, $currencyCodeType, $paymentType,
            $returnURL, $cancelURL);
$ack = strtoupper($resArray["ACK"]);
if($ack=="SUCCESS" || $ack=="SUCCESSWITHWARNING")
{
 RedirectToPayPal ( $resArray["TOKEN"] );
}
else
{
 //Display a user-friendly Error on the page using any of the following error information
 //returned by PayPal.
 $ErrorCode = urldecode($resArray["L_ERRORCODE0"]);
 $ErrorShortMsg = urldecode($resArray["L_SHORTMESSAGE0"]);
 $ErrorLongMsg = urldecode($resArray["L_LONGMESSAGE0"]);
 $ErrorSeverityCode = urldecode($resArray["L_SEVERITYCODE0"]);

 echo "SetExpressCheckout API call failed. ";
 echo "Detailed Error Message: " . $ErrorLongMsg;
 echo "Short Error Message: " . $ErrorShortMsg;
 echo "Error Code: " . $ErrorCode;
 echo "Error Severity Code: " . $ErrorSeverityCode;
}
?>
```

Example 2-3. billing.php

```
<?php

require_once ("paypalfunctions.php");

if ( $PaymentOption == "PayPal")
{
```

```
// ================================
// PayPal Express Checkout Module
// ================================

//'------------------------------------
//' The paymentAmount is the total value of
//' the shopping cart, which was set
//' earlier in a session variable
//' by the shopping cart page.
//'------------------------------------
$paymentAmount = $_SESSION["Payment_Amount"];

//'------------------------------------
//' When you integrate this code,
//' set the following variables with
//' shipping address details
//' entered by the user on the
//' Shipping page.
//'------------------------------------
$shipToName = "<<ShiptoName>>";
$shipToStreet = "<<ShipToStreet>>";
$shipToStreet2 = "<<ShipToStreet2>>"; //Leave it blank if there is no value
$shipToCity = "<<ShipToCity>>";
$shipToState = "<<ShipToState>>";
$shipToCountryCode = "<<ShipToCountryCode>>"; // Please refer to the PayPal country
                                              //codes in the API documentation.
$shipToZip = "<<ShipToZip>>";
$phoneNum = "<<PhoneNumber>>";

//'------------------------------------
//' The currencyCodeType and paymentType
//' are set to the selections made in the Integration Assistant.
//'------------------------------------
$currencyCodeType = "USD";
$paymentType = "Sale";

//'------------------------------------
//' The returnURL is the location where buyers return to when a
//' payment has been succesfully authorized.
//'
//' This is set to the value entered in the Integration Assistant.
//'------------------------------------
$returnURL = "http://www.michaelbalderas.com/paypal/expresscheckout/OrderConfirm.php";

//'------------------------------------
//' The cancelURL is the location buyers are sent to when they hit the
//' cancel button during authorization of payment during the PayPal flow.
//'
//' This is set to the value entered in the Integration Assistant.
//'------------------------------------
$cancelURL = "http://www.michaelbalderas.com/paypal/expresscheckout/shoppingcart.php";

//'------------------------------------
//' Calls the SetExpressCheckout API call
//'
```

```
//' The CallMarkExpressCheckout function is defined in the file PayPalFunctions.php,
//' it is included at the top of this file.
//'--------------------------------------------------
$resArray = CallMarkExpressCheckout ($paymentAmount, $currencyCodeType, $paymentType,
          $returnURL, $cancelURL, $shipToName, $shipToStreet, $shipToCity,
          $shipToState, $shipToCountryCode, $shipToZip, $shipToStreet2, $phoneNum
);

$ack = strtoupper($resArray["ACK"]);
if($ack=="SUCCESS" || $ack=="SUCCESSWITHWARNING")
{
 $token = urldecode($resArray["TOKEN"]);
 $_SESSION['reshash']=$token;
 RedirectToPayPal ( $token );
}
else
{
 //Display a user-friendly Error on the page using any of the
 //following error information returned by PayPal.
 $ErrorCode = urldecode($resArray["L_ERRORCODE0"]);
 $ErrorShortMsg = urldecode($resArray["L_SHORTMESSAGE0"]);
 $ErrorLongMsg = urldecode($resArray["L_LONGMESSAGE0"]);
 $ErrorSeverityCode = urldecode($resArray["L_SEVERITYCODE0"]);

 echo "SetExpressCheckout API call failed. ";
 echo "Detailed Error Message: " . $ErrorLongMsg;
 echo "Short Error Message: " . $ErrorShortMsg;
 echo "Error Code: " . $ErrorCode;
 echo "Error Severity Code: " . $ErrorSeverityCode;
 }
}
else
{
 if ((( $PaymentOption == "Visa") || ( $PaymentOption == "MasterCard") ||
   ($PaymentOption == "Amex") || ($PaymentOption == "Discover"))
   && ( $PaymentProcessorSelected == "PayPal Direct Payment"))

 //'-----------------------------------
 //' The paymentAmount is the total value of
 //' the shopping cart, which was set
 //' earlier in a session variable
 //' by the shopping cart page.
 //'-----------------------------------
 $paymentAmount = $_SESSION["Payment_Amount"];

 //'-----------------------------------
 //' The currencyCodeType and paymentType
 //' are set to the selections made in the Integration Assistant.
 //'-----------------------------------
 $currencyCodeType = "USD";
 $paymentType = "Sale";

 //' Set these values based on what was selected by the user on the
 //' Billing page Html form
```

```php
$creditCardType = "<<Visa/MasterCard/Amex/Discover>>"; //' Set this to one of the
                // acceptable values (Visa/MasterCard/Amex/Discover) match it to
                // what was selected on your Billing page.
$creditCardNumber = "<<CC number>>"; //' Set this to the string entered as the
                // credit card number on the Billing page.
$expDate = "<<Expiry Date>>"; //' Set this to the credit card expiry date
                // entered on the Billing page.
$cvv2 = "<<cvv2>>"; //' Set this to the CVV2 string entered on the Billing page
$firstName = "<<firstName>>"; //' Set this to the customer's first name that was entered
                // on the Billing page.
$lastName = "<<lastName>>"; //' Set this to the customer's last name that was entered on
                // the Billing page.
$street = "<<street>>"; //' Set this to the customer's street address that was entered on
                // the Billing page.
$city = "<<city>>"; //' Set this to the customer's city that was entered on
                // the Billing page.
$state = "<<state>>"; //' Set this to the customer's state that was entered
                // on the Billing page.
$zip = "<<zip>>"; //' Set this to the zip code of the customer's address that was
                // entered on the Billing page.
$countryCode = "<<PayPal Country Code>>"; //' Set this to the PayPal code for the
                //Country of the customer's address that was entered on the Billing page.
$currencyCode = "<<PayPal Currency Code>>"; //' Set this to the PayPal code for
                // the Currency used by the customer.

/*
'-----------------------------------------------
' Calls the DoDirectPayment API call
'
' The DirectPayment function is defined in PayPalFunctions.php, included at the top of
' this file.
'-----------------------------------------------
*/

$resArray = DirectPayment ( $paymentType, $paymentAmount, $creditCardType,
     $creditCardNumber, $expDate, $cvv2, $firstName, $lastName, $street,
     $city, $state, $zip, $countryCode, $currencyCode );

$ack = strtoupper($resArray["ACK"]);
if($ack=="SUCCESS" || $ack=="SUCCESSWITHWARNING")
{
//Getting transaction ID from API response.
 $TransactionID = urldecode9$resArray["TRANSACTIONID"]);

 echo "Your payment has been successfully processed";
}
else
{
//Display a user-friendly Error on the page using any of the following error information
//returned by PayPal.
$ErrorCode = urldecode($resArray["L_ERRORCODE0"]);
$ErrorShortMsg = urldecode($resArray["L_SHORTMESSAGE0"]);
$ErrorLongMsg = urldecode($resArray["L_LONGMESSAGE0"]);
$ErrorSeverityCode = urldecode($resArray["L_SEVERITYCODE0"]);
```

```
    echo "Direct credit card payment API call failed. ";
    echo "Detailed Error Message: " . $ErrorLongMsg;
    echo "Short Error Message: " . $ErrorShortMsg;
    echo "Error Code: " . $ErrorCode;
    echo "Error Severity Code: " . $ErrorSeverityCode;
  }
}
?>
```

Example 2-4. shipping.php

```php
<?php
/*===================================================================
 PayPal Express Checkout Call
 ===================================================================
*/
// Check to see whether the Request object contains a variable named 'token'.
$token = "";
if (isset($_REQUEST['token']))
{
  $token = $_REQUEST['token'];
}

// If the Request object contains the variable 'token', then it means that the
// user is coming from the PayPal site.
if ( $token != "" )
{

  require_once ("paypalfunctions.php");

  /*
  '----------------------------------
  ' Calls the GetExpressCheckoutDetails API call
  '
  ' The GetShippingDetails function is defined in PayPalFunctions.jsp,
  ' included at the top of this file.
  '------------------------------------------------
  */


  $resArray = GetShippingDetails( $token );
  $ack = strtoupper($resArray["ACK"]);
  if( $ack == "SUCCESS" || $ack == "SUCESSWITHWARNING")
  {
    /*
    ' The information that is returned by the GetExpressCheckoutDetails call should be
    ' integrated by the partner into his Order Review page.
    */
    $email = $resArray["EMAIL"]; // ' Email address of payer.
    $payerId = $resArray["PAYERID"]; // ' Unique PayPal customer account
                                     // identification number.
    $payerStatus = $resArray["PAYERSTATUS"]; // ' Status of payer.
                                             // Limited to 10 single-byte alphabetic
                                             // characters.
    $salutation = $resArray["SALUTATION"]; // ' Payer's salutation.
```

```php
        $firstName = $resArray["FIRSTNAME"]; // ' Payer's first name.
        $middleName = $resArray["MIDDLENAME"]; // ' Payer's middle name.
        $lastName = $resArray["LASTNAME"]; // ' Payer's last name.
        $suffix = $resArray["SUFFIX"]; // ' Payer's suffix.
        $cntryCode = $resArray["COUNTRYCODE"]; // ' Payer's country of residence in the form of
                                    // ISO standard 3166 two-character country codes.
        $business = $resArray["BUSINESS"]; // ' Payer's business name.
        $shipToName = $resArray["SHIPTONAME"]; // ' Person's name associated with this address.
        $shipToStreet = $resArray["SHIPTOSTREET"]; // ' First street address.
        $shipToStreet2 = $resArray["SHIPTOSTREET2"]; // ' Second street address.
        $shipToCity = $resArray["SHIPTOCITY"]; // ' Name of city.
        $shipToState = $resArray["SHIPTOSTATE"]; // ' State or province.
        $shipToCntryCode = $resArray["SHIPTOCOUNTRYCODE"]; // ' Country code.
        $shipToZip = $resArray["SHIPTOZIP"]; // ' U.S. Zip code or other country-specific
                                    // postal code.
        $addressStatus = $resArray["ADDRESSSTATUS"]; // ' Status of street address on file
                                    // with PayPal.
        $invoiceNumber = $resArray["INVNUM"]; // ' Your own invoice or tracking number, as set
                                    // by you in the element of the same name.
                                    //in SetExpressCheckout request.
        $phoneNumber = $resArray["PHONENUM"]; // ' Payer's contact telephone number. Note:
                                    // PayPal returns a contact telephone number only
                                    // if your Merchant account profile settings require
                                    // that the buyer enter one.
    }
    else
    {
    //Display a user-friendly Error on the page using any of the following error
    //information returned by PayPal.
    $ErrorCode = urldecode($resArray["L_ERRORCODE0"]);
    $ErrorShortMsg = urldecode($resArray["L_SHORTMESSAGE0"]);
    $ErrorLongMsg = urldecode($resArray["L_LONGMESSAGE0"]);
    $ErrorSeverityCode = urldecode($resArray["L_SEVERITYCODE0"]);

    echo "GetExpressCheckoutDetails API call failed. ";
    echo "Detailed Error Message: " . $ErrorLongMsg;
    echo "Short Error Message: " . $ErrorShortMsg;
    echo "Error Code: " . $ErrorCode;
    echo "Error Severity Code: " . $ErrorSeverityCode;
    }
}

?>
```

Example 2-5. orderconfirmation.php

```php
<?php
/*=================================================================
 PayPal Express Checkout Call
 =================================================================
*/
require_once ("paypalfunctions.php");

if ( $PaymentOption == "PayPal" )
{
```

```
/*
'-----------------------------------
' The paymentAmount is the total value of
' the shopping cart, which was set
' earlier in a session variable
' by the shopping cart page.
'-----------------------------------
*/

$finalPaymentAmount =  $_SESSION["Payment_Amount"];

/*
'-----------------------------------
' Calls the DoExpressCheckoutPayment API call
'
' The ConfirmPayment function is defined in the file PayPalFunctions.jsp,
' included at the top of this file.
'--------------------------------------------------
*/

$resArray = ConfirmPayment ( $finalPaymentAmount );
$ack = strtoupper($resArray["ACK"]);
if( $ack == "SUCCESS" || $ack == "SUCCESSWITHWARNING" )
{
 /*
 '***********************************************************************************
 '
 ' THE PARTNER SHOULD SAVE THE KEY TRANSACTION-RELATED INFORMATION SUCH AS
 '                   transactionId & orderTime
 '  IN THEIR OWN DATABASE AND THE REST OF THE INFORMATION
 '  CAN BE USED TO UNDERSTAND THE STATUS OF THE PAYMENT
 '
 '***********************************************************************************
 */

 $transactionId = $resArray["TRANSACTIONID"]; // ' Unique transaction ID of the payment.
 // Note:  If the PaymentAction of the request was Authorization or Order,
 // this value is your AuthorizationID for use with the Authorization &
 // Capture APIs.
 $transactionType = $resArray["TRANSACTIONTYPE"]; //' The type of transaction Possible
                                       // values: l cart l express-checkout
 $paymentType = $resArray["PAYMENTTYPE"];  //' Indicates whether the payment is instant
                                       // or delayed. Possible values: none,
                                       // echeck, instant
 $orderTime = $resArray["ORDERTIME"];  //' Time/date stamp of payment.
 $amt = $resArray["AMT"];  //' The final amount charged, including any shipping and
                           // taxes from your Merchant Profile.
 $currencyCode = $resArray["CURRENCYCODE"];  //' A three-character currency code for
                                       // one of the currencies listed in
                                       // PayPal-Supported Transactional
                                       // Currencies. Default: USD.
 $feeAmt = $resArray["FEEAMT"];  //' PayPal fee amount charged for the transaction
 $settleAmt = $resArray["SETTLEAMT"];  //' Amount deposited in your PayPal account
                                       // after a currency conversion.
 $taxAmt = $resArray["TAXAMT"];  //' Tax charged on the transaction.
```

```
$exchangeRate = $resArray["EXCHANGERATE"];  //' Exchange rate if a currency conversion
                                            // occurred. Relevant only if you are
                                            // billing in their non-primary currency.
                                            // If the customer chooses to pay with a
                                            // currency other than the non-primary
                                            // currency, the conversion occurs
                                            // in the customer's account.

/*
  'Status of the payment:
  'Completed: The payment has been completed, and the funds have been added
  'successfully to your account balance.
  'Pending: The payment is pending. See the PendingReason element for more information.
*/

$paymentStatus = $resArray["PAYMENTSTATUS"];

/*
'The reason the payment is pending:
'  none: No pending reason.
'  address: The payment is pending because your customer did not include a
'           confirmed shipping address and your Payment Receiving Preferences
'           is set such that you want to manually accept or deny each of these
'           payments. To change your preference, go to the Preferences section
'           of your Profile.
'  echeck: The payment is pending because it was made by an eCheck that has
'          not yet cleared.
'  intl: The payment is pending because you hold a non-U.S. account and
'        do not have a withdrawal mechanism. You must manually accept or
'        deny this payment from your Account Overview.
'  multi-currency: You do not have a balance in the currency sent,
'                  and you do not have your Payment Receiving
'                  Preferences set to automatically convert and
'                  accept this payment. You must manually accept
'                  or deny this payment.
'  verify: The payment is pending because you are not yet verified.
'          You must verify your account before you can accept this payment.
'  other: The payment is pending for a reason other than those listed above.
'         For more information, contact PayPal customer service.
*/

$pendingReason = $resArray["PENDINGREASON"];

/*
'The reason for a reversal if TransactionType is reversal:
'  none: No reason code.
'  chargeback: A reversal has occurred on this transaction due to a
'              chargeback by your customer.
'  guarantee: A reversal has occurred on this transaction due to
'             your customer triggering a money-back guarantee.
'  buyer-complaint: A reversal has occurred on this transaction
'                   due to a complaint about the transaction
'                   from your customer.
```

```
'   refund: A reversal has occurred on this transaction because
'            you have given the customer a refund.
'   other: A reversal has occurred on this transaction due to
'            a reason not listed above.
*/

$reasonCode = $resArray["REASONCODE"];
}
else
{
//Display a user-friendly Error on the page using any of the
//following error information returned by PayPal.
$ErrorCode = urldecode($resArray["L_ERRORCODE0"]);
$ErrorShortMsg = urldecode($resArray["L_SHORTMESSAGE0"]);
$ErrorLongMsg = urldecode($resArray["L_LONGMESSAGE0"]);
$ErrorSeverityCode = urldecode($resArray["L_SEVERITYCODE0"]);

echo "GetExpressCheckoutDetails API call failed. ";
echo "Detailed Error Message: " . $ErrorLongMsg;
echo "Short Error Message: " . $ErrorShortMsg;
echo "Error Code: " . $ErrorCode;
echo "Error Severity Code: " . $ErrorSeverityCode;
}
}

?>
```

Example 2-6. shoppingcart.php

```
<form action='expresscheckout.php' METHOD='POST'>
<input type='image' name='submit'
src='https://www.paypal.com/en_US/i/btn/btn_xpressCheckout.gif'
border='0' align='top' alt='Check out with PayPal'/>
</form>
```

CHAPTER 3

PayPal Website Payments Pro

PayPal's Website Payments Pro allows you API access to two components: Express Checkout (covered in Chapter 2) and Direct Payment. Direct Payment allows you to accept debit and credit cards directly from your site. Direct Payment, unlike Express Pay, requires the buyer to enter payment, billing, and shipping information, and does not require the buyer to have a PayPal Account. In addition, Website Payments Pro accounts do not show up as "PayPal" on your customer's credit card statements: your company's name shows up instead.

Overview of Direct Payment

Direct Payment allows your customers to pay via credit or debit cards during your checkout flow. This gives the seller complete control over the buyer's transaction experience. When a buyer chooses to pay with a credit or debit card, he enters his card number and other information directly on your site. This arrangement makes the seller/merchant responsible for maintaining the security of the transaction, rather than PayPal, and it is highly recommended that you provide the checkout experience under an SSL connection. After the buyer confirms his order and clicks the Pay button, you complete the transaction by invoking the `DoDirectPayment` API operation.

Direct Payment Workflow

Figure 3-1 shows the checkout workflow a user experiences with Direct Payment:

1. The buyer clicks the Checkout button on your website, provides shipping and billing information, and clicks Continue.
2. The buyer reviews the order for accuracy and clicks Pay.
3. Information is handed off to PayPal via the `DoDirectPayment` API operation, and the buyer's card is charged.
4. The customer receives the Order Complete summary page.

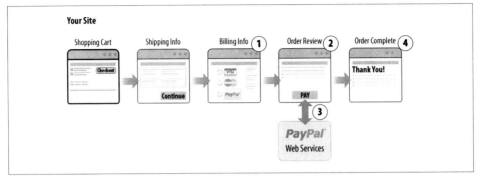

Figure 3-1. PayPal Direct Payment workflow

PayPal Direct Payment API Operations

The PayPal NVP API uses only one method related to Direct Payment: `DoDirectPayment`. This one method initializes the payment and returns the results all in one operation. Table 3-1 outlines the `DoDirectPayment` request fields, and Table 3-2 outlines the method's response fields.

Table 3-1. DoDirectPayment request fields

Field	Description
METHOD	Must be `DoDirectPayment` (required).
PAYMENTACTION	Indicates how you want to obtain payment:
	• `Authorization`: This payment is a basic authorization subject to settlement with PayPal Authorization and Capture.
	• `Sale`: This is the default value, indicating that it is a final sale.
	Limitation: Up to 13 single-byte characters.
IPADDRESS	The IP address of the buyer's browser (required). PayPal records this IP address to detect possible fraud. Limitation: Up to 15 single-byte characters, including periods. Must be an IPv4 address.
RETURNFMFDETAILS	Flag that indicates whether you want the results returned by the Fraud Management Filters:
	• `0`: Do not receive FMF details (default)
	• `1`: Receive FMF details
CREDITCARDTYPE	The type of credit card being used. Allowed values are:
	• `Visa`
	• `MasterCard`
	• `Discover`
	• `Amex`
	• `Maestro` *
	• `Solo` *

Field	Description
	* If using Maestro or Solo, the CURRENCYCODE must be GBP. Additionally, either START DATE or ISSUENUMBER must be specified.
	Limitation: Up to 10 single-byte alphabetic characters. For the UK, only Maestro, Solo, MasterCard, Discover, and Visa are allowed. For Canada, only MasterCard and Visa are allowed.
ACCT	The customer's credit card number. Limitations: Numeric characters only, with no spaces or punctuation. Must conform with the modulo and length required by each card type.
EXPDATE	The credit card expiration date, in the format MMYYYY. Limitations: Six single-byte alphanumeric characters, including the leading 0.
CVV2	The card verification value, version 2. This field may or may not be required, depending on your merchant account settings.
	The character length for Visa, MasterCard, and Discover is three digits. The character length for American Express is four digits. To adhere to credit card processing regulations, you cannot store this value after a transaction is complete.
STARTDATE	The month and year that a Maestro or Solo card was issued, in MMYYYY format. This value must be six digits, including the leading zero.
ISSUENUMBER	The issue number of a Maestro or Solo card. Two numeric digit maximum.
EMAIL	The email address of the buyer. Limited to 127 single-byte characters.
FIRSTNAME	The buyer's first name (required). Limited to 25 single-byte characters.
LASTNAME	The buyer's last name (required). Limited to 25 single-byte characters.
STREET	The first street address (required). Limited to 100 single-byte characters.
STREET2	The second street address (required). Limited to 100 single-byte characters.
CITY	The name of the city (required). Limited to 40 single-byte characters.
STATE	The state or province (required). Limited to 40 single-byte characters.
COUNTRYCODE	The country code (required). Limited to two single-byte characters.
ZIP	The U.S. zip code or another country-specific postal code (required). Limited to 20 single-byte characters.
SHIPTOPHONENUM	The phone number. Limited to 20 single-byte characters.
AMT	The total cost of the transaction to the customer (required).
	If the shipping cost and tax charges are known, include them in this value; if not, this value should be the current subtotal of the order. If the transaction includes one or more one-time purchases, this field must be equal to the sum of the purchases. Set this field to 0 if the transaction does not include a one-time purchase, for example, when you set up a billing agreement for a recurring payment that is not charged immediately. Purchase-specific fields will be ignored.
	Limitations: Must not exceed $10,000 USD in any currency. No currency symbol. Must have two decimal places, the decimal separator must be a period (.), and the optional thousands separator must be a comma (,).
CURRENCYCODE	A three-character currency code. The default is USD.

Field	Description
ITEMAMT	Sum of the cost of all items in this order. ITEMAMT is required if you specify L_AMTn. Limitations: Must not exceed $10,000 USD in any currency. No currency symbol. Must have two decimal places, the decimal separator must be a period (.), and the optional thousands separator must be a comma (,).
SHIPPINGAMT	Total shipping cost for this order. If you specify a value for SHIPPINGAMT, you are required to specify a value for ITEMAMT as well. Limitations: Must not exceed $10,000 USD in any currency. No currency symbol. Must have two decimal places, the decimal separator must be a period (.), and the optional thousands separator must be a comma (,).
HANDLINGAMT	Total handling costs for this order. If you specify a value for HANDLINGAMT, you are required to specify a value for ITEMAMT as well. Limitations: Must not exceed $10,000 USD in any currency. No currency symbol. Must have two decimal places, the decimal separator must be a period (.), and the optional thousands separator must be a comma (,).
TAXAMT	Sum of the tax for all items in this order. TAXAMT is required if you specify L_TAXAMTn. Limitations: Must not exceed $10,000 USD in any currency. No currency symbol. Must have two decimal places, the decimal separator must be a period (.), and the optional thousands separator must be a comma (,).
DESC	A description of the items the customer is purchasing. Limited to 127 single-byte alphanumeric characters.
CUSTOM	A free-form field for your own use. Limited to 256 single-byte alphanumeric characters.
INVNUM	Your own internal invoice or tracking number. Limited to 127 single-byte alphanumeric characters.
BUTTONSOURCE	An identification code for use by third-party applications to identify transactions. Limited to 32 single-byte alphanumeric characters.
L_NAMEn	The item name. Limited to 127 single-byte characters.
L_DESCn	The item description. Limited to 127 single-byte characters.
L_AMTn	The cost of the item. If you specify a value for L_AMTn, you must specify a value for ITEMAMT. Limitations: Must not exceed $10,000 USD in any currency. No currency symbol. Must have two decimal places, the decimal separator must be a period (.), and the optional thousands separator must be a comma (,).
L_NUMBERn	The item number. Limited to 127 single-byte characters.
L_QTYn	The item quantity. Can be any positive integer.
L_TAXAMTn	The item's sales tax. Limitations: Must not exceed $10,000 USD in any currency. No currency symbol. Must have two decimal places, the decimal separator must be a period (.), and the optional thousands separator must be a comma (,).
SHIPTONAME	The person's name associated with the shipping address. Required if using a shipping address. Limited to 32 single-byte characters.
SHIPTOSTREET	The first street address. Required if using a shipping address. Limited to 100 single-byte characters.
SHIPTOSTREET2	The second street address. Limited to 100 single-byte characters.
SHIPTOCITY	The name of the city. Required if using a shipping address. Limited to 40 single-byte characters.
SHIPTOSTATE	The state or province. Required if using a shipping address. Limited to 40 single-byte characters.

Field	Description
SHIPTOZIP	The U.S. zip code or other country-specific postal code. Required if using a U.S. shipping address and might be required for other countries. Limited to 20 single-byte characters.
SHIPTOCOUNTRY	The country code. Required if using a shipping address. Limited to two single-byte characters.
SHIPTOPHONENUM	The phone number. Limited to 20 single-byte characters.

Table 3-2. DoDirectPayment response fields

Field	Description
TRANSACTIONID	The unique transaction ID of the payment. If the PaymentAction of the request was Authorization, the value of TransactionID is your AuthorizationID for use with the Authorization and Capture API.
AMT	This value is the amount of the payment you specified in the DoDirectPayment request.
AVSCODE	The Address Verification System response code. Limited to one single-byte alphanumeric character.
CVV2MATCH	The results of the CVV2 check by PayPal.
L_FMF*filterIDn*	The filter ID, including the filter type (PENDING, REPORT, or DENY), the *filterID*, and the entry number, *n*, starting from 0. *filterID* is one of the following values: • 1 = AVS No Match • 2 = AVS Partial Match • 3 = AVS Unavailable/Unsupported • 4 = Card Security Code (CSC) Mismatch • 5 = Maximum Transaction Amount • 6 = Unconfirmed Address • 7 = Country Monitor • 8 = Large Order Number • 9 = Billing/Shipping Address Mismatch • 10 = Risky ZIP Code • 11 = Suspected Freight Forwarder Check • 12 = Total Purchase Price Minimum • 13 = IP Address Velocity • 14 = Risky Email Address Domain Check • 15 = Risky Bank Identification Number (BIN) Check • 16 = Risky IP address Range • 17 = PayPal Fraud Model
L_FMF*filterNAMEn*	The filter name, including the filter type, (PENDING, REPORT, or DENY), the *filterNAME*, and the entry number, *n*, starting from 0.

Simple Direct Payment Integration

To implement a Direct Payment transaction, you need to invoke the `DoDirectPayment` API and provide information to identify the buyer's credit or debit card and the amount of the payment. Setting up the transaction is accomplished through the following steps:

1. Specify the amount of the transaction, including the currency if it is not in U.S. dollars. You should specify the total amount of the transaction if it is known; otherwise, specify the subtotal.

   `AMT=amount`

   `CURRENCYCODE=currencyID`

2. Specify the payment action. It is best practice to explicitly specify the payment action as one of the following values:

   `PAYMENTACTION=Sale`

   `PAYMENTACTION=Authorization`

3. Specify the IP address of the buyer's computer:

   `IPADDRESS=xxx.xxx.xxx.xxx`

4. Specify information about the card being used. You must specify the type of card as well as the account number:

   `CREDITCARDTYPE=Visa`

   `ACCT=1234567891011123`

   The type of credit/debit card being used, the card issuer, and the Payment Receiving Preferences setting on your PayPal Profile might require that you set the following fields as well:

   `EXPDATE=012010`

   `CVV2=123`

5. Specify information about the card holder. You must provide the first and last name of the card holder, as well as the billing address associated with the card:

   `FIRSTNAME=John`

   `LASTNAME=Doe`

   `STREET=1313 Mockingbird Lane`

   `CITY=Any town`

   `STATE=Any state`

   `ZIP=11111`

   `COUNTRYCODE=US`

Direct Payment Integrations

Direct Payment is probably the easiest component to integrate for NVP access. You can add DoDirectPayment functionality to your checkout processor by adding the code in Example 3-1 and providing your API credentials. For instructions on creating those credentials, refer to "Creating an API Signature" on page 4. Additionally, after you have completed testing and are ready to go live, change `$environment = 'sandbox'` to `$environment='live'`.

Example 3-1. dodirectpayment.php

```php
<?php

/** DoDirectPayment NVP example; last modified 08MAY23.
 *
 *  Process a credit card payment.
 */

$environment = 'sandbox'; // or 'beta-sandbox' or 'live'

/**
 * Send HTTP POST Request
 *
 * @param string The API method name
 * @param string The POST Message fields in &name=value pair format
 * @return array Parsed HTTP Response body
 */
function PPHttpPost($methodName_, $nvpStr_) {
 global $environment;

 // Set up your API credentials, PayPal end point, and API version.
 $API_UserName = urlencode('my_api_username');
 $API_Password = urlencode('my_api_password');
 $API_Signature = urlencode('my_api_signature');
 $API_Endpoint = "https://api-3t.paypal.com/nvp";
 if("sandbox" === $environment || "beta-sandbox" === $environment) {
  $API_Endpoint = "https://api-3t.$environment.paypal.com/nvp";
 }
 $version = urlencode('51.0');

 // Set the curl parameters.
 $ch = curl_init();
 curl_setopt($ch, CURLOPT_URL, $API_Endpoint);
 curl_setopt($ch, CURLOPT_VERBOSE, 1);

 // Turn off the server and peer verification (TrustManager Concept).
 curl_setopt($ch, CURLOPT_SSL_VERIFYPEER, FALSE);
 curl_setopt($ch, CURLOPT_SSL_VERIFYHOST, FALSE);

 curl_setopt($ch, CURLOPT_RETURNTRANSFER, 1);
 curl_setopt($ch, CURLOPT_POST, 1);
```

```php
// Set the API operation, version, and API signature in the request.
$nvpreq = "METHOD=$methodName_&VERSION=$version&PWD=$API_Password&USER=$API_UserName".
        "&SIGNATURE=$API_Signature$nvpStr_";

// Set the request as a POST FIELD for curl.
curl_setopt($ch, CURLOPT_POSTFIELDS, $nvpreq);

// Get response from the server.
$httpResponse = curl_exec($ch);

if(!$httpResponse) {
exit("$methodName_ failed: ".curl_error($ch).'('.curl_errno($ch).')');
}

// Extract the response details.
$httpResponseAr = explode("&", $httpResponse);

$httpParsedResponseAr = array();
foreach ($httpResponseAr as $i => $value) {
$tmpAr = explode("=", $value);
if(sizeof($tmpAr) > 1) {
 $httpParsedResponseAr[$tmpAr[0]] = $tmpAr[1];
 }
}

if((0 == sizeof($httpParsedResponseAr))||!array_key_exists('ACK', $httpParsedResponseAr))
{
 exit("Invalid HTTP Response for POST request($nvpreq) to $API_Endpoint.");
}

 return $httpParsedResponseAr;
}

// Set request-specific fields.
$paymentType = urlencode('Authorization'); // or 'Sale'
$firstName = urlencode('customer_first_name');
$lastName = urlencode('customer_last_name');
$creditCardType = urlencode('customer_credit_card_type');
$creditCardNumber = urlencode('customer_credit_card_number');
$expDateMonth = 'cc_expiration_month';
// Month must be padded with leading zero
$padDateMonth = urlencode(str_pad($expDateMonth, 2, '0', STR_PAD_LEFT));

$expDateYear = urlencode('cc_expiration_year');
$cvv2Number = urlencode('cc_cvv2_number');
$address1 = urlencode('customer_address1');
$address2 = urlencode('customer_address2');
$city = urlencode('customer_city');
$state = urlencode('customer_state');
$zip = urlencode('customer_zip');
$country = urlencode('customer_country'); // US or other valid country code
$amount = urlencode('example_payment_amuont');
$currencyID = urlencode('USD'); // or other currency ('GBP', 'EUR', 'JPY', 'CAD', 'AUD')
```

```php
// Add request-specific fields to the request string.
$nvpStr ="&PAYMENTACTION=$paymentType&AMT=$amount&CREDITCARDTYPE=$creditCardType".
    "&ACCT=$creditCardNumber&EXPDATE=$padDateMonth$expDateYear&CVV2=$cvv2Number".
    "&FIRSTNAME=$firstName&LASTNAME=$lastName&STREET=$address1&CITY=$city".
    "&STATE=$state&ZIP=$zip&COUNTRYCODE=$country&CURRENCYCODE=$currencyID";

// Execute the API operation; see the PPHttpPost function above.
$httpParsedResponseAr = PPHttpPost('DoDirectPayment', $nvpStr);

if("SUCCESS" == strtoupper($httpParsedResponseAr["ACK"])||"SUCCESSWITHWARNING"==
    strtoupper($httpParsedResponseAr["ACK"])) {
 exit('Direct Payment Completed Successfully: '.print_r($httpParsedResponseAr, true));
} else  {
 exit('DoDirectPayment failed: ' . print_r($httpParsedResponseAr, true));
}

?>
```

CHAPTER 4

PayPal Adaptive Payments

Overview of Adaptive Payments

PayPal's Adaptive Payments allow you to send money in a variety of scenarios. Using Adaptive Payments, you can build a "send money" application for a social networking site or build a robust payment system. Through the Adaptive Payments API, you can build an application that can handle payments, payment preapprovals, and refunds. You can also create foreign currency exchange rates for a set list of amounts, which then allows you to build a payment interface that shows the buyer her order total in different currencies (e.g., U.S. dollars and euros).

Another advantage of Adaptive Payments is that you can be an application owner—for example, an online merchant who owns a website, a payment application provider for cell phones, or a widget developer of a payments widget on a social networking site—without assuming the responsibility of sending or receiving the transactions.

PayPal Adaptive Payments API Operations Overview

Adaptive Payments is made up of 10 key API operations, listed in Table 4-1.

Table 4-1. Adaptive Payments API operations

API operation	Description
CancelPreapproval	Cancels a preapproval
ConvertCurrency	Obtains foreign exchange currency conversion rates for a list of amounts
ExecutePayment	Executes a payment
GetPaymentOptions	Obtains the settings specified with the SetPaymentOptions API operation
Pay	Transfers fund from a sender's (buyer's) PayPal account to on or more receivers' PayPal accounts (up to six recipients)
PaymentDetails	Obtains information about a payment set up with the Pay API operation

API operation	Description
Preapproval	Sets up preapprovals, which is an approval to make future payments on the sender's behalf
PreapprovalDetails	Obtains information about a preapproval
Refund	Refunds all or part of a payment
SetPaymentOptions	Sets payment options

Adaptive Payments Permission Levels

PayPal's Adaptive Payments adds an additional layer of security and permission levels over other API functionality. Most of the Adaptive Payments API operations are available to all API callers, but some of the higher-level features are limited to those with advanced permission levels.

A merchant using a third-party Adaptive Payments application, at minimum, must have the same permission level required for the Adaptive Payments APIs called by the application. If, for example, your application supports chained payments but the merchant using it has a standard permission level, chained payments will not work for that merchant. Table 4-2 outlines the current permission restrictions. This list is subject to change, and so I suggest referring to *http://www.paypal.com* or *http://www.x.com* for more information about current permission levels.

 If you are distributing an application based upon Adaptive Payments, I highly recommend putting the required permission levels in your application distribution notes.

Table 4-2. Adaptive Payments permission levels and allowed features

Standard permission level	Advanced permission level
Simple and parallel payments with explicit approval	Chained payments
Get payment details	Payments with implicit approval
Refunds	Preapprovals and preapproval cancellations
Currency conversion	Get preapproval details
	Pay request with CREATE action type
	SetPaymentOptions API operation
	GetPaymentOptions API operation
	ExecutePayment API operation
	Personal payments

Adaptive Payments Application Workflows

Adaptive Payments facilitates payments between a sender and one or more receivers of that payment. You as the application owner and your application are the caller of the Adaptive Payments API operations. The application owner must have a PayPal business-level account, but senders and receivers can have a PayPal account of any type. Given the complexity and power for Adaptive Payments, you can be both the application owner and the receiver of payments. Outlined in Figure 4-1, this is referred to as a simple payment, where a sender makes a payment to a single recipient. This type of payment is equivalent to what is done with Express Checkout.

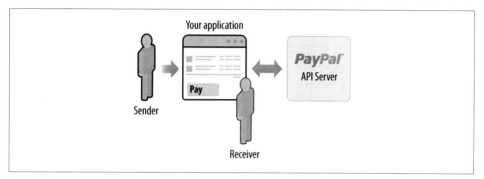

Figure 4-1. Adaptive Payments owner as recipient workflow

The Adaptive Payments API allows you and your application to act as an intermediary that facilitates payments for others, without you being a recipient of the funds, as outlined in Figure 4-2. This is referred to as a *parallel payment*, in which the sender transmits a single payment to multiple recipients and can see who those recipients are. Parallel payments are commonly used in aggregated shopping, and allow a customer to order from multiple vendors with a single shopping cart.

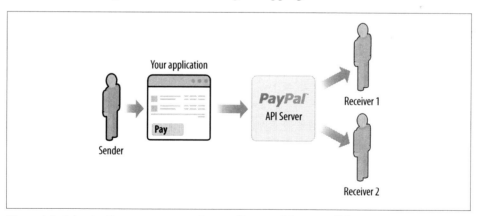

Figure 4-2. Adaptive Payments owner as intermediary workflow: parallel

Another way in which your application can function as an intermediary is facilitating a *chained payment*, outlined in Figure 4-3. In a chained transaction, your application receives the payment, and the funds are then split between multiple recipients on the backend. In a chained setup, your application can take a percentage off the top and then disperse the remaining funds to the other recipients. You can even set up what is called a *delayed chained payment*. This can be used when your secondary receivers are required to ship goods, for example, before they receive their payment for the transaction.

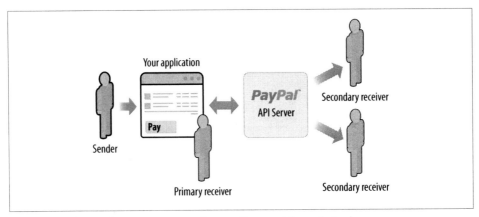

Figure 4-3. Adaptive Payments owner as intermediary workflow: chained

And finally, your application also can be the sender of the transaction, outlined in Figure 4-4. This could be used to facilitate commission payments to your sales reps, for example.

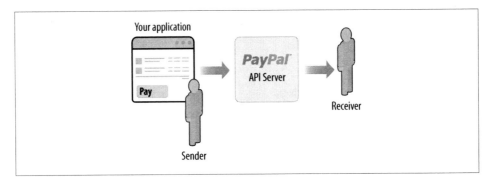

Figure 4-4. Adaptive Payments application as sender

So, as you can see from these workflow diagrams and notes, Adaptive Payments is probably the most powerful payment method PayPal provides to application developers.

Payment Approval and Payment Flows

Once a payment transaction via your application has been submitted, the sender of the payment must take an additional step and approve the transfer of funds. This can be one of four different payment approval types: Explicit, Preapproved, Implicit, or Guest Payments.

Explicit Payments

Explicit Payments require the sender to log into PayPal.com (*http://www.paypal.com/*) and approve each individual payment. This is the traditional method for paying via PayPal and is the only option a sender has, unless he has previously set up a preapproval agreement with you, or unless the sender is also the application provider. You can control the interaction between your application and PayPal during the transaction process by providing URLs for redirecting the sender, dependent on the situation. Figure 4-5 outlines an Explicit Payment flow, which consists of the following steps:

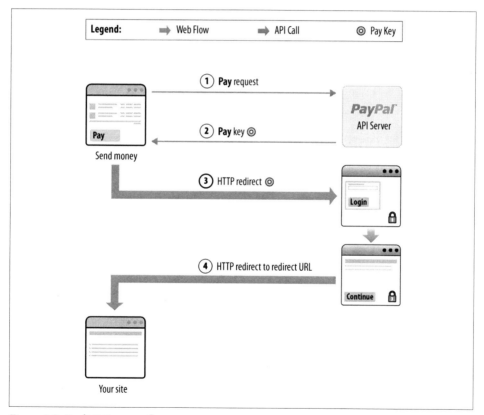

Figure 4-5. Explicit Payment flow

1. Your application sends a **Pay** request to PayPal.
2. PayPal responds with a key that you use to redirect the sender to PayPal.
3. You redirect the sender to PayPal.com (*http://www.paypal.com/*).
4. The sender approves the transfer of the payment, and PayPal redirects the sender to a URL you specify.
5. PayPal sends both you and the sender an email summarizing the payment that was made.

Preapproved Payments

Preapproved Payments require senders to log into PayPal.com (*http://www.paypal .com/*) and set up preapprovals for future payments, for example, payments to a supplier they use frequently. Once the preapproval is set up, payments automatically are considered approved, and the sender will not have to log in to approve payments to that vendor in the future. During the preapproval setup process, the sender can specify the following:

- Duration of the preapproval, including the start date and end date. This comes in handy if you are paying a specific vendor for supplies on a particular project that has a known start and end date, for example.
- The maximum amount being approved at one time.
- The maximum number of payments allowed for the vendor.

Figure 4-6 outlines a Preapproved Payment flow, which consists of the following steps:

1. Your application sends a preapproval request to PayPal.
2. PayPal responds with a key, called a preapproval key, that you use in redirecting the sender to PayPal. If the preapproval has already been established, you will use this key to complete payments automatically on the sender's behalf.
3. You redirect the sender to PayPal.
4. After the sender approves the preapproval, PayPal redirects the sender to a URL you specify.
5. PayPal sends both you and the sender an email summarizing the payment that was made.

Once the sender approves the preapproval setup, you can make payments on behalf of the sender directly, as outlined in Figure 4-7:

1. Your application sends a **Pay** request to PayPal that includes a preapproval key identifying the payment agreement.
2. PayPal responds with a payment key that you can use for other API functions.

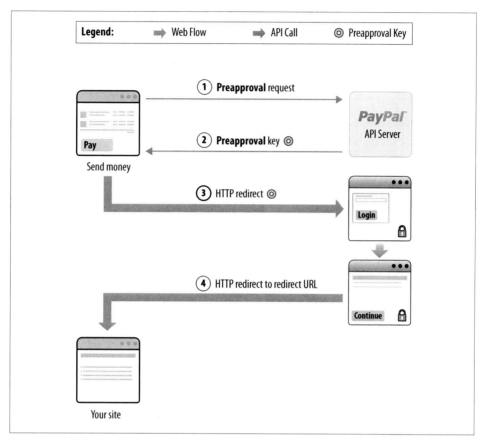

Figure 4-6. Preapproved Payment flow

Figure 4-7. Preapproved Payment direct sending

Implicit Payments

Implicit Payments are payments sent directly by your application in which the sender and API caller are using the same PayPal account. Since your account is the one sending the payments, no approval is necessary for the payment transaction. Figure 4-8 outlines an Implicit Payment:

1. Your application sends a **Pay** request to PayPal.
2. PayPal responds with a key to use for other API operations.

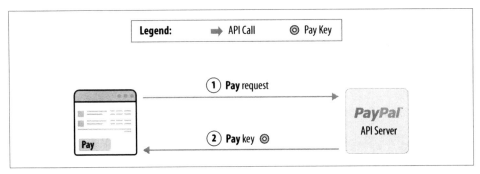

Figure 4-8. Implicit Payment flow

Guest Payments

Adaptive Payments also supports Guest Payments, where the sender can pay using her credit card, similar to using Direct Payment. The recipient must have either a business- or premier-level PayPal account. Guest Payments are handled in the same manner as Explicit Payments, except that the sender provides credit card information directly on the PayPal payment screen.

Adaptive Payments API Operations in Depth

In the remaining pages of this chapter, we look at the following Adaptive Payments API operations in depth:

- Pay API
- SetPaymentOptions API
- ExecutePayment API

A complete list of all the defined Adaptive Payments API operations can be found at *http://developer.paypal.com* or *http://x.com*.

Pay API Operation

All payments made via Adaptive Payments have the same required fields. These are outlined in Table 4-3.

Table 4-3. Common required fields

Field	Description
actionType	Will be one of three possible values:
	• PAY: Use this value if not using the request in combination with Execute PaymentRequest.
	• CREATE: Use to set up payment instructions with a SetPaymentOptions request and then execute at a later time with an ExecutePaymentRequest.
	• PAY_PRIMARY: Used for chained payments only. This allows you to delay payments to secondary receivers at the time of the transaction and process only the primary receiver. To process the secondary payments, initiate Execute PaymentRequest and pass the pay key obtained from the PayResponse.
receiverList.receiver(*n*).email	The receiver's email address.
receiverList.receiver(*n*).amount	The amount to be credited to the receiver's account.
currencyCode	The code for the currency in which the payment is made. You can specify only one currency, regardless of the number of receivers.
cancelUrl	The URL for sender redirection if the sender cancels the payment approval. This value is required, but used only for explicit payments.
returnUrl	The URL for sender redirection after completion of the payment. This value is required, but used only for explicit payments.
requestEnvelope.errorLanguage	The code for the language used when returning errors (must be en_US).

If you are performing a parallel payment, you must provide the additional fields outlined in Table 4-4.

Table 4-4. Parallel payments fields

Field	Description
receiverList.receiver(*n*).email	The email address for each receiver. *n* is an integer between 0 and 5, allowing for a maximum of six receivers.
receiverList.receiver(*n*).amount	The amount to send to each corresponding receiver.

If you are performing a chained payment, you must provide the additional fields outlined in Table 4-5.

Table 4-5. Chained payments fields

Field	Description
receiverList.receiver(*n*).email	The email address for each receiver. *n* is an integer between 0 and 5, for a total of one primary receiver and one to five secondary receivers.
receiverList.receiver(*n*).amount	The amount to send to each corresponding receiver.
receiverList.receiver(*n*).primary	Set this value to true to indicate that this is a chained payment. Only one receiver can be the primary receiver.

As discussed previously, a payment requires explicit approval by default. To initiate the approval process, your application must redirect the sender to PayPal as follows:

https://www.paypal.com/webscr?cmd=_ap-payment&paykey=value

If you are the API caller and you specify your email address in the senderEmail field, PayPal will implicitly approve the payment without redirecting to PayPal. You can also use a preapproval to execute the payment and avoid explicit approval. The required preapproval fields are outlined in Table 4-6.

Table 4-6. Preapproval fields

Field	Description
preapprovalKey	Preapproval key for the approval set up between you and the sender
pin	Sender's personal identification number, if one was specified when the approval agreement was created

SetPaymentOptions API Operation

The SetPaymentOptions API is used to specify settings for a payment of the actionType CREATE. SetPaymentOptions has four different request fields, outlined in Table 4-7.

Table 4-7. SetPaymentOptionsRequest fields

Field	Descriptions
displayOptions	The container used to specify which images should be used when emailing customers.
initiatingEntity	The PayPal financial partner initiating the payment. These must be set up via the Admin tool prior to using the PayPal APIs.
payKey	This field identifies the payment for which you wish to set up payment options. This is the key that is returned in the PayResponse message.
requestEnvelope	This is required information common to each API operation. This would include things such as the language in which error messages are displayed.

Next, we look at the different request fields and their additional values.

displayOptions

displayOptions has two optional fields that you can specify, outlined in Table 4-8.

Table 4-8. displayOptions fields

Field	Description
emailHeaderImageUrl	The URL that points to the location of the image used in the header of customer emails. The image dimensions are 43 pixels high x 240 pixels wide.
emailMarketingImageUrl	The URL that points to the location of the marketing image used in customer emails. The image dimensions are 80 pixels high x 530 pixels wide.

initiatingEntity

initiatingEntity has only one optional field, outlined in Table 4-9.

Table 4-9. initiatingEntity field

Field	Description
institutionCustomer	Details about the party that initiated this payment. This payment is made by the API caller on behalf of the initiating party. The initiating party can be an institution or a customer of that institution. The initiating party must be set up by PayPal Merchant Services.

institutionCustomer has the additional fields outlined in Table 4-10.

Table 4-10. institutionCustomer fields

Field	Description
countryCode	The two-character country code of the end user's home country (required)
displayName	The full name of the consumer as known by the institution (required)
email	The email address of the consumer as known by the institution
firstName	The first name of the consumer as known by the institution (required)
institutionCustomerId	The unique identifier assigned to the consumer by the institution (required)
institutionId	The unique identifier assigned to the institution (required)
lastName	The last name of the consumer as known by the institution (required)

requestEnvelope

requestEnvelope has two fields, outlined in Table 4-11.

Table 4-11. requestEnvelope fields

Field	Description
detailLevel	The level of detail required by the client application for components such as Item and Transaction. One possible value is ReturnAll, which provides the maximum level of detail (default).
errorLanguage	The RFC 3066 language in which error messages are returned (required). By default, it is en_US, which is the only language currently supported.

ResponseEnvelope

Once you execute your `SetPaymentOptions` request, you will receive a `ResponseEnve
lope` that contains information about the success or failure of the `SetPaymentOptions`
request. The response fields are outlined in Table 4-12.

Table 4-12. SetPaymentOptions response fields

Field	Description
ack	The acknowledgment code. Possible values are:
	• `Success`: The operation completed successfully.
	• `Failure`: The operation failed.
	• `Warning`: Warning.
	• `SuccessWithWarning`: The operation completed successfully, but there is a warning message.
	• `FailureWithWarning`: The operation failed with a warning message.
build	The build number; used only by Developer Technical Support.
correlationId	The correlation ID; used only by Developer Technical Support.
timestamp	The date on which the response was sent. The time currently is not supported.

ExecutePayment API Operation

The `ExecutePayment` API operation allows you to execute a payment setup with the
Pay API operation using the `actionType` `CREATE`. The request is comprised of two fields,
outlined in Table 4-13.

Table 4-13. ExecutePayment request fields

Field	Description
payKey	The pay key that identifies the payment to be executed. This is the pay key returned in the PayResponse message.
requestEnvelope	Information common to each API operation, such as the language in which an error message is returned.

Additionally, `requestEnvelope` contains two subfields, outlined in Table 4-14.

Table 4-14. requestEnvelope fields

Field	Description
detailLevel	The level of detail required by the client application for components such as Item and Transaction. One possible value is `ReturnAll`, which provides the maximum level of detail (default).
errorLanguage	The RFC 3066 language in which error messages are returned (required). By default, it is en_US, which is the only language currently supported.

`ExecutePayment` returns several elements in its response, outlined in Table 4-15.

Table 4-15. ExecutePayment response fields

Field	Description
payErrorList	Information about why a payment failed.
paymentExecStatus	The status of the payment. Possible values are:
	• CREATED: The payment request was received, and funds will be transferred once the payment is approved.
	• COMPLETED: The payment was successful.
	• INCOMPLETE: Some transfers succeeded and some failed for a parallel payment.
	• ERROR: The payment failed, and either all attempted transfers failed or all completed transfers were successfully reversed.
	• REVERSALERROR: One or more transfers failed when attempting to reverse a payment.
responseEnvelope	Common response information, including a timestamp and the response acknowledgment status.

Additional values and information related to the `ExecutePayment` response fields can be found in the online documentation located at *http://www.x.com/community/ppx/documentation.*

Adaptive Payments Integration

PayPal provides an Integration Wizard for Adaptive Payments as well. It can be found at *https://www.paypal-labs.com/integrationwizard/adaptive/main.php.* The wizard for Adaptive Payments contains only five steps.

The Integration Wizard starts by presenting an overview of the different types of payment methods you can implement via Adaptive Payments, as shown in Figure 4-9.

Step 1 asks you for your programming language and whether you are working with the sandbox or a live implementation (see Figure 4-10).

Step 2 allows you to download the *paypalplatform.php* code, shown in Example 4-1 (see Figure 4-11). This code contains all the core handlers for Adaptive Payments information. You will need to provide your API credentials in this file. For instructions on creating those credentials, refer to "Creating an API Signature" on page 4. Once you have completed your testing and are ready to go live, change `$Env="sandbox"` to `$Env="live"`. This will change the endpoint to the live PayPal endpoint.

Figure 4-9. Adaptive Payments Integration Wizard overview

Step 3 generates the code to implement for your Preapproval Flow handler, shown in Example 4-2 (see Figure 4-12).

Step 4 generates the different payment type handlers for use in your code (see Figure 4-13). You will have an Implicit Payment handler (Example 4-3), a Basic Payment Handler (Example 4-4), a Parallel Payment Handler (Example 4-5), and a Chained Payment Handler (Example 4-6).

Step 5 completes the Integration Wizard, as shown in Figure 4-14.

Figure 4-10. Adaptive Payments Integration Wizard step 1

Figure 4-11. Adaptive Payments Integration Wizard step 2

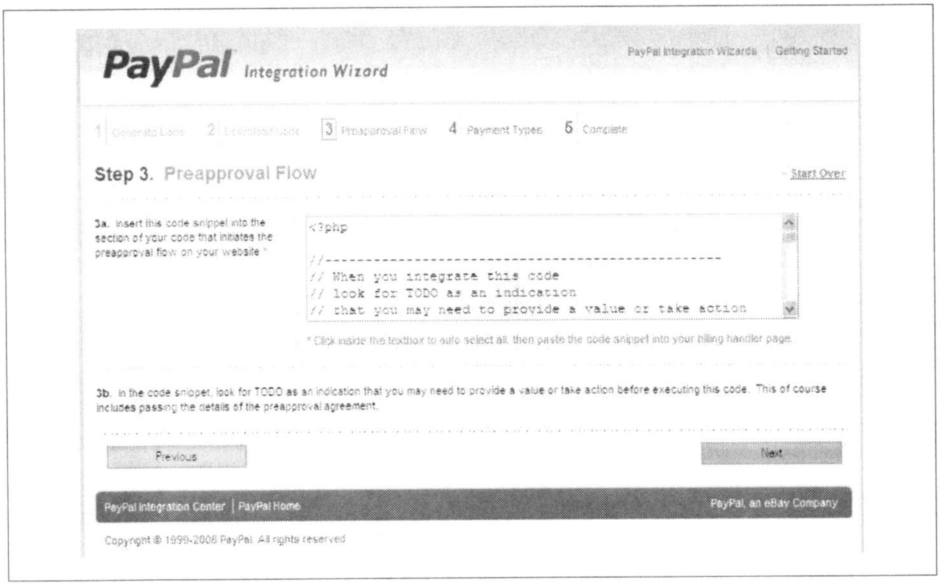

Figure 4-12. *Adaptive Payments Integration Wizard step 3*

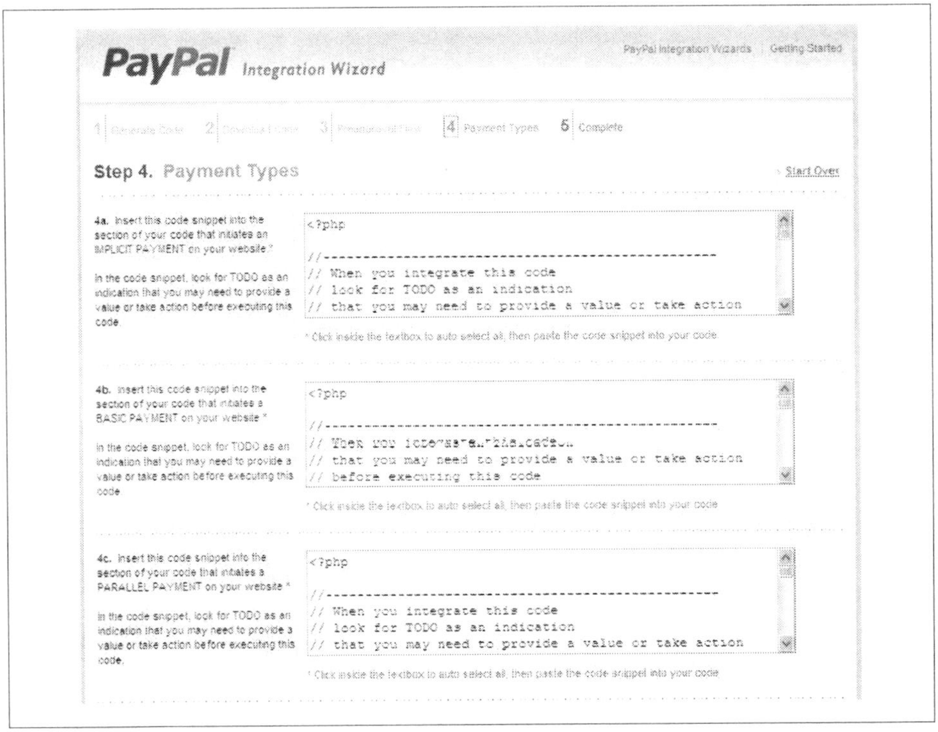

Figure 4-13. *Adaptive Payments Integration Wizard step 4*

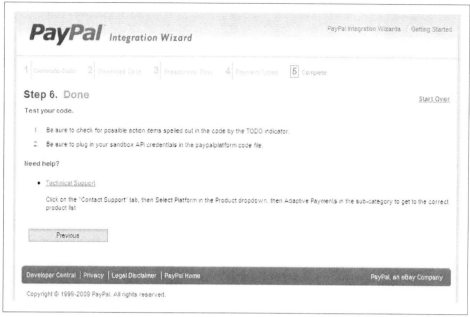

Figure 4-14. Adaptive Payments Integration Wizard step 5

Example 4-1. paypalplatform.php

```php
<?php
/*********************************************
PayPal Adaptive Payments API Module

Defines all the global variables and the wrapper functions
*********************************************/
$PROXY_HOST = '127.0.0.1';
$PROXY_PORT = '808';

$Env = "sandbox";

//-----------------------------------
// PayPal API Credentials
// Replace <API_USERNAME> with your API Username
// Replace <API_PASSWORD> with your API Password
// Replace <API_SIGNATURE> with your Signature
//-----------------------------------
$API_UserName = "<API_USERNAME>";
$API_Password = "<API_PASSWORD>";
$API_Signature = "<API_SIGNATURE>";
// AppID is preset for sandbox use
//    If your application goes live, you will be assigned a value for the live
//    environment by PayPal as part of the live onboarding process.
$API_AppID = "APP-80W284485P519543T";
$API_Endpoint = "";
```

```php
if ($Env == "sandbox")
{
 $API_Endpoint = "https://svcs.sandbox.paypal.com/AdaptivePayments";
}
else
{
 $API_Endpoint = "https://svcs.paypal.com/AdaptivePayments";
}

$USE_PROXY = false;

if (session_id() == "")
 session_start();

function generateCharacter () {
 $possible = "1234567890abcdefghijklmnopqrstuvwxyzABCDEFGHIJKLMNOPQRSTUVWXYZ";
 $char = substr($possible, mt_rand(0, strlen($possible)-1), 1);
 return $char;
}

function generateTrackingID () {
$GUID = generateCharacter().generateCharacter().generateCharacter();
$GUID .=generateCharacter().generateCharacter().generateCharacter();
$GUID .=generateCharacter().generateCharacter().generateCharacter();
return $GUID;
}

/*
'-----------------------------------------------------------------------------
' Purpose: Prepares the parameters for the Refund API Call.
'    The API credentials used in a Pay call can make the Refund call
'    against a payKey, or a tracking id, or to specific receivers of a payKey or
'    a tracking id that resulted from the Pay call.
'
'    A receiver itself with its own API credentials can make a Refund call against
'    the transactionId corresponding to their transaction.
'    The API credentials used in a Pay call cannot use transactionId to issue a refund
'    for a transaction for which they themselves were not the receiver.
'
'    If you do specify specific receivers, you must provide the amounts as well.
'    If you specify a transactionId, then only the receiver of that transactionId
'    is affected. Therefore the receiverEmailArray and receiverAmountArray should
'    have 1 entry each if you do want to give a partial refund.
' Inputs:
'
' Conditionally Required:
'  One of the following: payKey or trackingId or trasactionId or
'                        (payKey and receiverEmailArray and receiverAmountArray) or
'                        (trackingId and receiverEmailArray and receiverAmountArray)
'                        or (transactionId and receiverEmailArray
'                        and receiverAmountArray)
' Returns:
'  The NVP Collection object of the Refund call response.
'-----------------------------------------------------------------------------
*/
```

```php
function CallRefund( $payKey, $transactionId, $trackingId,
        $receiverEmailArray, $receiverAmountArray )
{
/* Gather the information to make the Refund call.
 The variable nvpstr holds the name-value pairs.
*/

$nvpstr = "";

// conditionally required fields
if ("" != $payKey)
{
 $nvpstr = "payKey=" . urlencode($payKey);
 if (0 != count($receiverEmailArray))
 {
  reset($receiverEmailArray);
  while (list($key, $value) = each($receiverEmailArray))
  {
   if ("" != $value)
   {
    $nvpstr .= "&receiverList.receiver(" . $key . ").email=" . urlencode($value);
   }
  }
 }
 if (0 != count($receiverAmountArray))
 {
  reset($receiverAmountArray);
  while (list($key, $value) = each($receiverAmountArray))
  {
   if ("" != $value)
   {
    $nvpstr .= "&receiverList.receiver(" . $key . ").amount=" . urlencode($value);
   }
  }
 }
}
elseif ("" != $trackingId)
{
 $nvpstr = "trackingId=" . urlencode($trackingId);
 if (0 != count($receiverEmailArray))
 {
  reset($receiverEmailArray);
  while (list($key, $value) = each($receiverEmailArray))
  {
   if ("" != $value)
   {
    $nvpstr .= "&receiverList.receiver(" . $key . ").email=" . urlencode($value);
   }
  }
 }
 if (0 != count($receiverAmountArray))
 {
  reset($receiverAmountArray);
  while (list($key, $value) = each($receiverAmountArray))
  {
```

```
   if ("" != $value)
   {
    $nvpstr .= "&receiverList.receiver(" . $key . ").amount=" . urlencode($value);
   }
  }
 }
}
elseif ("" != $transactionId)
{
 $nvpstr = "transactionId=" . urlencode($transactionId);
 // the caller should only have 1 entry in the email and amount arrays
 if (0 != count($receiverEmailArray))
 {
  reset($receiverEmailArray);
  while (list($key, $value) = each($receiverEmailArray))
  {
   if ("" != $value)
   {
    $nvpstr .= "&receiverList.receiver(" . $key . ").email=" . urlencode($value);
   }
  }
 }
 if (0 != count($receiverAmountArray))
 {
  reset($receiverAmountArray);
  while (list($key, $value) = each($receiverAmountArray))
  {
   if ("" != $value)
   {
    $nvpstr .= "&receiverList.receiver(" . $key . ").amount=" . urlencode($value);
   }
  }
 }
}

/* Make the Refund call to PayPal */
$resArray = hash_call("Refund", $nvpstr);

/* Return the response array */
return $resArray;
}

/*
'-------------------------------------------------------------------------------
' Purpose: Prepares the parameters for the PaymentDetails API Call.
'   The PaymentDetails call can be made with either
'   a payKey, a trackingId, or a transactionId of a previously successful Pay call.
' Inputs:
'
' Conditionally Required:
'   One of the following:  payKey or transactionId or trackingId
' Returns:
'   The NVP Collection object of the PaymentDetails call response.
'-------------------------------------------------------------------------------
*/
```

```
function CallPaymentDetails( $payKey, $transactionId, $trackingId )
{
 /* Gather the information to make the PaymentDetails call.
  The variable nvpstr holds the name-value pairs.
 */

 $nvpstr = "";

 // conditionally required fields
 if ("" != $payKey)
 {
  $nvpstr = "payKey=" . urlencode($payKey);
 }
 elseif ("" != $transactionId)
 {
  $nvpstr = "transactionId=" . urlencode($transactionId);
 }
 elseif ("" != $trackingId)
 {
  $nvpstr = "trackingId=" . urlencode($trackingId);
 }

 /* Make the PaymentDetails call to PayPal */
 $resArray = hash_call("PaymentDetails", $nvpstr);

 /* Return the response array */
 return $resArray;
}

/*
'-------------------------------------------------------------------------------
' Purpose:    Prepares the parameters for the Pay API Call.
' Inputs:
'
' Required:
'
' Optional:
'
' Returns:
'  The NVP Collection object of the Pay call response.
'-------------------------------------------------------------------------------
*/
function CallPay( $actionType, $cancelUrl, $returnUrl, $currencyCode,
    $receiverEmailArray, $receiverAmountArray, $receiverPrimaryArray,
    $receiverInvoiceIdArray, $feesPayer, $ipnNotificationUrl, $memo,
    $pin, $preapprovalKey, $reverseAllParallelPaymentsOnError,
    $senderEmail, $trackingId )
{
 /* Gather the information to make the Pay call.
  The variable nvpstr holds the name-value pairs.
 */
```

```php
// required fields
$nvpstr = "actionType=" . urlencode($actionType) . "&currencyCode=";
$nvpstr .= urlencode($currencyCode) . "&returnUrl=";
$nvpstr .= urlencode($returnUrl) . "&cancelUrl=" . urlencode($cancelUrl);

if (0 != count($receiverAmountArray))
{
 reset($receiverAmountArray);
 while (list($key, $value) = each($receiverAmountArray))
 {
  if ("" != $value)
  {
   $nvpstr .= "&receiverList.receiver(" . $key . ").amount=" . urlencode($value);
  }
 }
}

if (0 != count($receiverEmailArray))
{
 reset($receiverEmailArray);
 while (list($key, $value) = each($receiverEmailArray))
 {
  if ("" != $value)
  {
   $nvpstr .= "&receiverList.receiver(" . $key . ").email=" . urlencode($value);
  }
 }
}

if (0 != count($receiverPrimaryArray))
{
 reset($receiverPrimaryArray);
 while (list($key, $value) = each($receiverPrimaryArray))
 {
  if ("" != $value)
  {
   $nvpstr = $nvpstr . "&receiverList.receiver(" . $key . ").primary=" .
        urlencode($value);
  }
 }
}

if (0 != count($receiverInvoiceIdArray))
{
 reset($receiverInvoiceIdArray);
 while (list($key, $value) = each($receiverInvoiceIdArray))
 {
  if ("" != $value)
  {
   $nvpstr = $nvpstr . "&receiverList.receiver(" . $key . ").invoiceId=" .
        urlencode($value);
  }
 }
}
```

```php
// optional fields
if ("" != $feesPayer)
{
  $nvpstr .= "&feesPayer=" . urlencode($feesPayer);
}

if ("" != $ipnNotificationUrl)
{
  $nvpstr .= "&ipnNotificationUrl=" . urlencode($ipnNotificationUrl);
}

if ("" != $memo)
{
  $nvpstr .= "&memo=" . urlencode($memo);
}

if ("" != $pin)
{
  $nvpstr .= "&pin=" . urlencode($pin);
}

if ("" != $preapprovalKey)
{
  $nvpstr .= "&preapprovalKey=" . urlencode($preapprovalKey);
}

if ("" != $reverseAllParallelPaymentsOnError)
{
  $nvpstr .= "&reverseAllParallelPaymentsOnError=";
  $nvpstr .= urlencode($reverseAllParallelPaymentsOnError);
}

if ("" != $senderEmail)
{
  $nvpstr .= "&senderEmail=" . urlencode($senderEmail);
}

if ("" != $trackingId)
{
  $nvpstr .= "&trackingId=" . urlencode($trackingId);
}

/* Make the Pay call to PayPal */
$resArray = hash_call("Pay", $nvpstr);

/* Return the response array */
return $resArray;
}

/*
'-------------------------------------------------------------------------
' Purpose: Prepares the parameters for the PreapprovalDetails API Call.
' Inputs:
'
```

```
'   Required:
'   preapprovalKey:A preapproval key that identifies the agreement
'                  resulting from a previously successful Preapproval call.
'   Returns:
'   The NVP Collection object of the PreapprovalDetails call response.
'-----------------------------------------------------------------------
*/
function CallPreapprovalDetails( $preapprovalKey )
{
 /* Gather the information to make the PreapprovalDetails call.
  The variable nvpstr holds the name-value pairs.
 */

 // required fields
 $nvpstr = "preapprovalKey=" . urlencode($preapprovalKey);

 /* Make the PreapprovalDetails call to PayPal */
 $resArray = hash_call("PreapprovalDetails", $nvpstr);

 /* Return the response array */
 return $resArray;
}

/*
'-----------------------------------------------------------------------
'   Purpose: Prepares the parameters for the Preapproval API Call.
'   Inputs:
'
'   Required:
'
'   Optional:
'
'   Returns:
'   The NVP Collection object of the Preapproval call response.
'-----------------------------------------------------------------------
*/
function CallPreapproval( $returnUrl, $cancelUrl, $currencyCode,
       $startingDate, $endingDate, $maxTotalAmountOfAllPayments,
       $senderEmail, $maxNumberOfPayments, $paymentPeriod, $dateOfMonth,
       $dayOfWeek, $maxAmountPerPayment, $maxNumberOfPaymentsPerPeriod, $pinType )
{
 /* Gather the information to make the Preapproval call.
  The variable nvpstr holds the name-value pairs.
 */

 // required fields
 $nvpstr = "returnUrl=" . urlencode($returnUrl) . "&cancelUrl=" . urlencode($cancelUrl);
 $nvpstr .= "&currencyCode=" . urlencode($currencyCode) . "&startingDate=";
 $nvpstr .= urlencode($startingDate) . "&endingDate=" . urlencode($endingDate);
 $nvpstr .= "&maxTotalAmountOfAllPayments=" . urlencode($maxTotalAmountOfAllPayments);

 // optional fields
 if ("" != $senderEmail)
 {
  $nvpstr .= "&senderEmail=" . urlencode($senderEmail);
```

```
    }

    if ("" != $maxNumberOfPayments)
    {
     $nvpstr .= "&maxNumberOfPayments=" . urlencode($maxNumberOfPayments);
    }

    if ("" != $paymentPeriod)
    {
     $nvpstr .= "&paymentPeriod=" . urlencode($paymentPeriod);
    }

    if ("" != $dateOfMonth)
    {
     $nvpstr .= "&dateOfMonth=" . urlencode($dateOfMonth);
    }

    if ("" != $dayOfWeek)
    {
     $nvpstr .= "&dayOfWeek=" . urlencode($dayOfWeek);
    }

    if ("" != $maxAmountPerPayment)
    {
     $nvpstr .= "&maxAmountPerPayment=" . urlencode($maxAmountPerPayment);
    }

    if ("" != $maxNumberOfPaymentsPerPeriod)
    {
     $nvpstr .= "&maxNumberOfPaymentsPerPeriod=" . urlencode($maxNumberOfPaymentsPerPeriod);
    }

    if ("" != $pinType)
    {
     $nvpstr .= "&pinType=" . urlencode($pinType);
    }

    /* Make the Preapproval call to PayPal */
    $resArray = hash_call("Preapproval", $nvpstr);

    /* Return the response array */
    return $resArray;
}

/**
  '-------------------------------------------------------------------------------
  * hash_call: Function to perform the API call to PayPal using API signature
  * @methodName is name of API method.
  * @nvpStr is nvp string.
  * returns an associative array containing the response from the server.
  '-------------------------------------------------------------------------------
*/
function hash_call($methodName, $nvpStr)
{
```

```php
//declaring of global variables
global $API_Endpoint, $API_UserName, $API_Password, $API_Signature, $API_AppID;
global $USE_PROXY, $PROXY_HOST, $PROXY_PORT;

$API_Endpoint .= "/" . $methodName;
//setting the curl parameters.
$ch = curl_init();
curl_setopt($ch, CURLOPT_URL,$API_Endpoint);
curl_setopt($ch, CURLOPT_VERBOSE, 1);

//turning off the server and peer verification(TrustManager Concept).
curl_setopt($ch, CURLOPT_SSL_VERIFYPEER, FALSE);
curl_setopt($ch, CURLOPT_SSL_VERIFYHOST, FALSE);

curl_setopt($ch, CURLOPT_RETURNTRANSFER,1);
curl_setopt($ch, CURLOPT_POST, 1);

// Set the HTTP Headers
curl_setopt($ch, CURLOPT_HTTPHEADER,  array(
'X-PAYPAL-REQUEST-DATA-FORMAT: NV',
'X-PAYPAL-RESPONSE-DATA-FORMAT: NV',
'X-PAYPAL-SECURITY-USERID: ' . $API_UserName,
'X-PAYPAL-SECURITY-PASSWORD: ' .$API_Password,
'X-PAYPAL-SECURITY-SIGNATURE: ' . $API_Signature,
'X-PAYPAL-SERVICE-VERSION: 1.3.0',
'X-PAYPAL-APPLICATION-ID: ' . $API_AppID
));

   //if USE_PROXY constant set to TRUE in Constants.php,
   //then only proxy will be enabled.
//Set proxy name to PROXY_HOST and port number to PROXY_PORT in constants.php
if($USE_PROXY)
 curl_setopt ($ch, CURLOPT_PROXY, $PROXY_HOST. ":" . $PROXY_PORT);

// RequestEnvelope fields
$detailLevel = urlencode("ReturnAll"); // See DetailLevelCode in the WSDL
                                       // for valid enumerations
$errorLanguage = urlencode("en_US");  // This should be the standard RFC
                                       // 3066 language identification tag,
                                       // e.g., en_US

// NVPRequest for submitting to server
$nvpreq = "requestEnvelope.errorLanguage=$errorLanguage&requestEnvelope";
$nvpreq .= "detailLevel=$detailLevel&$nvpStr";

 //setting the nvpreq as POST FIELD to curl
 curl_setopt($ch, CURLOPT_POSTFIELDS, $nvpreq);

 //getting response from server
 $response = curl_exec($ch);

 //converting NVPResponse to an Associative Array
 $nvpResArray=deformatNVP($response);
 $nvpReqArray=deformatNVP($nvpreq);
 $_SESSION['nvpReqArray']=$nvpReqArray;
```

```php
  if (curl_errno($ch))
  {
   // moving to display page to display curl errors
     $_SESSION['curl_error_no']=curl_errno($ch) ;
     $_SESSION['curl_error_msg']=curl_error($ch);

     //Execute the Error handling module to display errors.
  }
  else
  {
    //closing the curl
    curl_close($ch);
  }

  return $nvpResArray;
}
/*'---------------------------------------------------------------------
 Purpose: Redirects to PayPal.com site.
 Inputs:  $cmd is the querystring
 Returns:
 --------------------------------------------------------------------
*/
function RedirectToPayPal ( $cmd )
{
 // Redirect to paypal.com here
 global $Env;

 $payPalURL = "";

 if ($Env == "sandbox")
 {
  $payPalURL = "https://www.sandbox.paypal.com/webscr?" . $cmd;
 }
 else
 {
  $payPalURL = "https://www.paypal.com/webscr?" . $cmd;
 }

 header("Location: ".$payPalURL);
}


/*'---------------------------------------------------------------------
  * This function will take NVPString and convert it to an Associative Array
  * and then will decode the response.
  * It is useful to search for a particular key and display arrays.
  * @nvpstr is NVPString.
  * @nvpArray is Associative Array.
   ----------------------------------------------------------------
  */
```

```php
function deformatNVP($nvpstr)
{
 $intial=0;
 $nvpArray = array();

 while(strlen($nvpstr))
 {
  //postion of Key
  $keypos= strpos($nvpstr,'=');
  //position of value
  $valuepos = strpos($nvpstr,'&') ? strpos($nvpstr,'&'): strlen($nvpstr);

  /*getting the Key and Value values and storing in a Associative Array*/
  $keyval=substr($nvpstr,$intial,$keypos);
  $valval=substr($nvpstr,$keypos+1,$valuepos-$keypos-1);
  //decoding the respose
  $nvpArray[urldecode($keyval)] =urldecode( $valval);
  $nvpstr=substr($nvpstr,$valuepos+1,strlen($nvpstr));
      }
  return $nvpArray;
 }
?>
```

Example 4-2. preapprovalflow.php

```php
<?php

//-------------------------------------------------
// When you integrate this code,
// look for TODO as an indication
// that you may need to provide a value or take
// action before executing this code.
//-------------------------------------------------

require_once ("paypalplatform.php");


// ===================================
// PayPal Platform Preapproval Module
// ===================================

// Request specific required fields
$cancelUrl = "http://wwww.yoursite.com/PreapprovalCancelHandler.xxx";
            // TODO - The landing page on your site where the customer
            // is sent when they cancel the Preapproval action on PayPal
$returnUrl = "http://wwww.yoursite.com/PreapprovalReturnHandler.xxx";
            // TODO - The landing page on your site where the customer
            // returns to after the Preapproval is agreed to on PayPal
$currencyCode = "USD";
$startingDate = "2009-06-17T13:00:00"; // TODO - The datetime when this
                                       // preapproval agreement starts,
                                       // cannot be in the past
$endingDate = "2009-09-17T13:00:00"; // TODO - The datetime when this
                                     // preapproval agreement ends
```

```
$maxTotalAmountOfAllPayments = "2000"; // TODO - The maximum total amount
                                       // of all payments, cannot exceed
                                       // $2,000 USD or the equivalent
                                       // in other currencies

// Request specific optional fields
//   Provide a value for each field that you want to include in the request;
//   if left as an empty string, the field will not be passed in the request.
$senderEmail = ""; // TODO - The PayPal account email address of the sender
$maxNumberOfPayments = ""; // TODO - The maximum number of payments for
                           // this preapproval
$paymentPeriod = ""; // TODO - If this preapproval is for periodic payments,
                     // this defines the payment period as one of the following:
                     //    NO_PERIOD_SPECIFIED
                     //    DAILY - each day
                     //    WEEKLY - each week
                     //    BIWEEKLY - every other week
                     //    SEMIMONTHLY - twice a month
                     //    MONTHLY - each month
                     //    ANNUALLY - each year
$dateOfMonth = ""; // TODO - The day of the month on which a monthly payment is
                   // to be made, number between 1 and 31
$dayOfWeek = ""; // TODO - The day of the week that a weekly payment is to be
                 // made, see DayOfWeek in the WSDL for valid enumerations
$maxAmountPerPayment = ""; // TODO - The maximum amount per payment, it
                           //cannot exceed the value in maxTotalAmountOfAllPayments
$maxNumberOfPaymentsPerPeriod = ""; // TODO - The maximum number of all
                                    // payments per period
$pinType = ""; // TODO - Whether or not a personal identification number (PIN)
               // is required each time a Payment is made via the Pay API call
               //    NOT_REQUIRED - a PIN is not required (default)
               //    REQUIRED - a PIN is required; the sender must specify a PIN
               //      when setting up the preapproval on PayPal, and the PIN must
               //      be in the request of each subsequent Pay API call corresponding
               //      to this preapproval
               // A PIN is typically required if a Pay call against the preapproval
               // can be made for a purchase or payment in which the sender takes an
               // explicit action to send the money.

//-------------------------------------------------
// Make the Preapproval API call
//
// The CallPreapproval function is defined in the paypalplatform.php file,
// which is included at the top of this file.
//-------------------------------------------------
$resArray = CallPreapproval ($returnURL, $cancelURL, $currencyCode, $startingDate,
       $endingDate, $maxTotalAmountOfAllPayments, $senderEmail,
       $maxNumberOfPayments, $paymentPeriod, $dateOfMonth, $dayOfWeek,
       $maxAmountPerPayment, $maxNumberOfPaymentsPerPeriod, $pinType
);
```

```php
$ack = strtoupper($resArray["responseEnvelope.ack"]);
if($ack=="SUCCESS")
{
 $cmd = "cmd=_ap-preapproval&preapprovalkey=" . urldecode($resArray["preapprovalKey"]);
 RedirectToPayPal ( $cmd );
}
else
{
 //Display a user-friendly Error on the page using any of the following error information
 //returned by PayPal.
 //TODO - There can be more than 1 error, so check for "error(1).errorId",
 //then "error(2).errorId", and so on until you find no more errors.
 $ErrorCode = urldecode($resArray["error(0).errorId"]);
 $ErrorMsg = urldecode($resArray["error(0).message"]);
 $ErrorDomain = urldecode($resArray["error(0).domain"]);
 $ErrorSeverity = urldecode($resArray["error(0).severity"]);
 $ErrorCategory = urldecode($resArray["error(0).category"]);

 echo "Preapproval API call failed. ";
 echo "Detailed Error Message: " . $ErrorMsg;
 echo "Error Code: " . $ErrorCode;
 echo "Error Severity: " . $ErrorSeverity;
 echo "Error Domain: " . $ErrorDomain;
 echo "Error Category: " . $ErrorCategory;
}

?>
```

Example 4-3. implicitpayment.php

```php
<?php

//-------------------------------------------------
// When you integrate this code,
// look for TODO as an indication
// that you may need to provide a value or take
// action before executing this code.
//-------------------------------------------------

require_once ("paypalplatform.php");


// ================================
// PayPal Platform Implicit Payment Module
// ================================

// Request specific required fields
$senderEmail = "";  // TODO - The PayPal account email address of the sender
                    // Think of it as required for an implicit payment and
                    // set to the same account that owns the API credentials
$actionType = "PAY";
$cancelUrl = "https://NoOp";    // There is no approval step for implicit payment
$returnUrl = "https://NoOp";    // There is no approval step for implicit payment
$currencyCode = "USD";
```

```
// An implicit payment can be a simple or parallel or chained payment
// TODO - Specify the receiver emails
//          Remove or set to an empty string the array entries for receivers
//          that you do not have for a simple payment, specify only
//          receiver0email, and remove the other array entries
$receiverEmailArray = array(
  'receiver0email',
  'receiver1email',
  'receiver2email',
  'receiver3email',
  'receiver4email',
  'receiver5email'
  );

// TODO - Specify the receiver amounts as the amount of money,
//          for example, '5' or '5.55'. Remove or set to an empty
//          string the array entries for receivers that you do not have
//          for a simple payment, specify only receiver0amount, and remove
//          the other array entries
$receiverAmountArray = array(
  'receiver0amount',
  'receiver1amount',
  'receiver2amount',
  'receiver3amount',
  'receiver4amount',
  'receiver5amount'
  );

// TODO - Specify values ONLY if you are doing a chained payment
//          If you are doing a chained payment, then set ONLY 1 receiver in the
//          array to 'true' as the primary receiver, and set the other receivers
//          corresponding to those indicated in receiverEmailArray to 'false'
//          Make sure that you do NOT specify more values
//          in this array than in the receiverEmailArray
$receiverPrimaryArray = array(
  '',
  '',
  '',
  '',
  '',
  ''
  );

// TODO - Set invoiceId to uniquely identify the transaction
//          associated with each receiver
//          Set the array entries with value for receivers that you have
//          Each of the array values must be unique
$receiverInvoiceIdArray = array(
  '',
  '',
  '',
  '',
  '',
  ''
  );
```

```
// Request specific optional fields
//    Provide a value for each field that you want to include in the
//    request; if left as an empty string, the field will not be passed
//    in the request.
$feesPayer = ""; // For an implicit payment use case, this cannot be "SENDER"
$ipnNotificationUrl = "";
$memo = ""; // maxlength is 1000 characters
$pin = ""; // No pin for an implicit payment use case
$preapprovalKey = ""; // No preapprovalKey for an implicit use case
$reverseAllParallelPaymentsOnError = ""; // Only specify if you are doing a
                                         //parallel payment as your implicit
                                         //payment
$trackingId = generateTrackingID(); // generateTrackingID function is found
                                    // in paypalplatform.php


//-------------------------------------------------
// Make the Pay API call
//
// The CallPay function is defined in the paypalplatform.php file,
// which is included at the top of this file.
//-------------------------------------------------
$resArray = CallPay ($actionType, $cancelUrl, $returnUrl, $currencyCode,
     $receiverEmailArray, $receiverAmountArray, $receiverPrimaryArray,
     $receiverInvoiceIdArray, $feesPayer, $ipnNotificationUrl, $memo,
     $pin, $preapprovalKey, $reverseAllParallelPaymentsOnError,
     $senderEmail, $trackingId
);

$ack = strtoupper($resArray["responseEnvelope.ack"]);
if($ack=="SUCCESS")
{
 // payKey is the key that you can use to identify the payment resulting
 // from the Pay call.
 $payKey = urldecode($resArray["payKey"]);
 // paymentExecStatus is the status of the payment
 $paymentExecStatus = urldecode($resArray["paymentExecStatus"]);
}
else
{
 //Display a user-friendly Error on the page using any of the following
 //error information returned by PayPal.
 //TODO - There can be more than 1 error, so check for "error(1).errorId",
 // then "error(2).errorId", and so on until you find no more errors.
 $ErrorCode = urldecode($resArray["error(0).errorId"]);
 $ErrorMsg = urldecode($resArray["error(0).message"]);
 $ErrorDomain = urldecode($resArray["error(0).domain"]);
 $ErrorSeverity = urldecode($resArray["error(0).severity"]);
 $ErrorCategory = urldecode($resArray["error(0).category"]);

 echo "Preapproval API call failed. ";
 echo "Detailed Error Message: " . $ErrorMsg;
 echo "Error Code: " . $ErrorCode;
```

```php
  echo "Error Severity: " . $ErrorSeverity;
  echo "Error Domain: " . $ErrorDomain;
  echo "Error Category: " . $ErrorCategory;
}
?>
```

Example 4-4. basicpayment.php

```php
<?php

//-------------------------------------------------
// When you integrate this code,
// look for TODO as an indication
// that you may need to provide a value or take
// action before executing this code.
//-------------------------------------------------

require_once ("paypalplatform.php");


// ===================================
// PayPal Platform Basic Payment Module
// ===================================

// Request specific required fields
$actionType = "PAY";
$cancelUrl = "https://mycancelurl"; // TODO - If you are not executing the Pay call
                                    // for a preapproval, then you must set a valid
                                    // cancelUrl for the web approval flow that
                                    // immediately follows this Pay call
$returnUrl = "https://myreturnurl"; // TODO - If you are not executing the Pay call
                                    // for a preapproval, then you must set a valid
                                    // returnUrl for the web approval flow that
                                    // immediately follows this Pay call
$currencyCode = "USD";

// A basic payment has 1 receiver.
// TODO - specify the receiver email
$receiverEmailArray = array(
 'receiver0email'
 );

// TODO - specify the receiver amount as the amount of money, for example, '5' or '5.55'
$receiverAmountArray = array(
 'receiver0amount'
 );

// For basic payment, no primary indicators are needed, so set empty array.
$receiverPrimaryArray = array();

// TODO - Set invoiceId to uniquely identify the transaction associated with the receiver
//  You can set this to the same value as trackingId if you wish
$receiverInvoiceIdArray = array(
  '1234abcd'
  );
```

```
// Request specific optional or conditionally required fields
//    Provide a value for each field that you want to include in the request;
//    If left as an empty string, the field will not be passed in the request
$senderEmail = ""; // TODO - If you are executing the Pay call against a
                   //        preapprovalKey, you should set senderEmail
                   //        It is not required if the web approval flow immediately
                   //        follows this Pay call
$feesPayer = "";
$ipnNotificationUrl = "";
$memo = ""; // maxlength is 1000 characters
$pin = ""; // TODO - If you are executing the Pay call against an
           //        existing preapproval that requires a pin, then you
           //        must set this
$preapprovalKey = ""; // TODO - If you are executing the Pay call
                      //        against an existing preapproval, set the
                      //        preapprovalKey here
$reverseAllParallelPaymentsOnError = ""; // Do not specify for basic payment
$trackingId = generateTrackingID(); // generateTrackingID function is
                                    // found in paypalplatform.php


//--------------------------------------------------
// Make the Pay API call
//
// The CallPay function is defined in the paypalplatform.php file,
// which is included at the top of this file.
//--------------------------------------------------
$resArray = CallPay ($actionType, $cancelUrl, $returnUrl, $currencyCode,
      $receiverEmailArray, $receiverAmountArray, $receiverPrimaryArray,
      $receiverInvoiceIdArray, $feesPayer, $ipnNotificationUrl, $memo,
      $pin, $preapprovalKey, $reverseAllParallelPaymentsOnError,
      $senderEmail, $trackingId
);

$ack = strtoupper($resArray["responseEnvelope.ack"]);
if($ack=="SUCCESS")
{
 if ("" == $preapprovalKey)
 {
  // redirect for web approval flow
  $cmd = "cmd=_ap-payment&paykey=" . urldecode($resArray["payKey"]);
  RedirectToPayPal ( $cmd );
 }
 else
 {
  // payKey is the key that you can use to identify the payment resulting
  // from the Pay call.
  $payKey = urldecode($resArray["payKey"]);
  // paymentExecStatus is the status of the payment
 $paymentExecStatus = urldecode($resArray["paymentExecStatus"]);
 }
}
else
{
 //Display a user-friendly Error on the page using any of the following
 //error information returned by PayPal.
```

```php
//TODO - There can be more than 1 error, so check for "error(1).errorId",
//        then "error(2).errorId", and so on until you find no more errors.
$ErrorCode = urldecode($resArray["error(0).errorId"]);
$ErrorMsg = urldecode($resArray["error(0).message"]);
$ErrorDomain = urldecode($resArray["error(0).domain"]);
$ErrorSeverity = urldecode($resArray["error(0).severity"]);
$ErrorCategory = urldecode($resArray["error(0).category"]);

echo "Preapproval API call failed. ";
echo "Detailed Error Message: " . $ErrorMsg;
echo "Error Code: " . $ErrorCode;
echo "Error Severity: " . $ErrorSeverity;
echo "Error Domain: " . $ErrorDomain;
echo "Error Category: " . $ErrorCategory;
}
?>
```

Example 4-5. parallelpayment.php

```php
<?php

//-------------------------------------------------
// When you integrate this code,
// look for TODO as an indication
// that you may need to provide a value or take
// action before executing this code.
//-------------------------------------------------

require_once ("paypalplatform.php");


// =================================
// PayPal Platform Parallel Payment Module
// =================================

// Request specific required fields
$actionType = "PAY";
$cancelUrl = "https://mycancelurl"; // TODO - If you are not executing the Pay call
                                    // for a preapproval, then you must set a valid
                                    // cancelUrl for the web approval flow that
                                    // immediately follows this Pay call
$returnUrl = "https://myreturnurl"; // TODO - If you are not executing the Pay call
                                    // for a preapproval, then you must set a valid
                                    // returnUrl for the web approval flow that
                                    // immediately follows this Pay call
$currencyCode = "USD";

// A parallel payment can be made among two to six receivers
// TODO - Specify the receiver emails
//        Remove or set to an empty string the array entries for receivers that you
//        do not have
$receiverEmailArray = array(
  'receiver0email',
  'receiver1email',
  'receiver2email',
```

```php
  'receiver3email',
  'receiver4email',
  'receiver5email'
);

// TODO - Specify the receiver amounts as the amount of money, for example, '5' or '5.55'
//        Remove or set to an empty string the array entries for receivers that you
//        do not have
$receiverAmountArray = array(
  'receiver0amount',
  'receiver1amount',
  'receiver2amount',
  'receiver3amount',
  'receiver4amount',
  'receiver5amount'
);

// For parallel payment, no primary indicators are needed, so set empty array.
$receiverPrimaryArray = array();

// TODO - Set invoiceId to uniquely identify the transaction associated with
//        each receiver
//        Set the array entries with value for receivers that you have
//        Each of the array values must be unique
$receiverInvoiceIdArray = array(
  '',
  '',
  '',
  '',
  '',
  '',
  ''
);

// Request specific optional fields
//    Provide a value for each field that you want to include in the request;
//    if left as an empty string, the field will not be passed in the request
$senderEmail = ""; // TODO - If you are executing the Pay call against a
                   // preapprovalKey, you should set senderEmail
                   // It is not required if the web approval flow immediately
                   // follows this Pay call
$feesPayer = "";
$ipnNotificationUrl = "";
$memo = ""; // maxlength is 1000 characters
$pin = ""; // TODO - If you are executing the Pay call against an existing
           // preapproval that requires a pin, then you must set this
$preapprovalKey = ""; // TODO - If you are executing the Pay call against
                      // an existing preapproval, set the preapprovalKey here
$reverseAllParallelPaymentsOnError = ""; // TODO - Set this to "true" if you would
                                         // like each parallel payment to be reversed
                                         // if an error occurs
                                         // Defaults to "false" if you don't specify
$trackingId = generateTrackingID(); // generateTrackingID function is found
                                    // in paypalplatform.php
```

```php
//-------------------------------------------------
// Make the Pay API call
//
// The CallPay function is defined in the paypalplatform.php file,
// which is included at the top of this file.
//-------------------------------------------------
$resArray = CallPay ($actionType, $cancelUrl, $returnUrl, $currencyCode,
        $receiverEmailArray, $receiverAmountArray, $receiverPrimaryArray,
        $receiverInvoiceIdArray, $feesPayer, $ipnNotificationUrl, $memo,
        $pin, $preapprovalKey, $reverseAllParallelPaymentsOnError,
        $senderEmail, $trackingId
);

$ack = strtoupper($resArray["responseEnvelope.ack"]);
if($ack=="SUCCESS")
{
 if ("" == $preapprovalKey)
 {
  // redirect for web approval flow
  $cmd = "cmd=_ap-payment&paykey=" . urldecode($resArray["payKey"]);
  RedirectToPayPal ( $cmd );
 }
 else
 {
  // payKey is the key that you can use to identify the result from this Pay call
  $payKey = urldecode($resArray["payKey"]);
  // paymentExecStatus is the status of the payment
  $paymentExecStatus = urldecode($resArray["paymentExecStatus"]);
 }
}
else
{
 //Display a user-friendly Error on the page using any of the following error
 //information returned by PayPal.
 //TODO - There can be more than 1 error, so check for "error(1).errorId",
 //       then "error(2).errorId", and so on until you find no more errors.
 $ErrorCode = urldecode($resArray["error(0).errorId"]);
 $ErrorMsg = urldecode($resArray["error(0).message"]);
 $ErrorDomain = urldecode($resArray["error(0).domain"]);
 $ErrorSeverity = urldecode($resArray["error(0).severity"]);
 $ErrorCategory = urldecode($resArray["error(0).category"]);

 echo "Preapproval API call failed. ";
 echo "Detailed Error Message: " . $ErrorMsg;
 echo "Error Code: " . $ErrorCode;
 echo "Error Severity: " . $ErrorSeverity;
 echo "Error Domain: " . $ErrorDomain;
 echo "Error Category: " . $ErrorCategory;
}
?>
```

Example 4-6. chainedpayment.php

```php
<?php

//-----------------------------------------------
// When you integrate this code,
// look for TODO as an indication
// that you may need to provide a value or take
// action before executing this code.
//-----------------------------------------------

require_once ("paypalplatform.php");


// ===================================
// PayPal Platform Chained Payment Module
// ===================================

// Request specific required fields
$actionType = "PAY";
$cancelUrl = "https://mycancelurl"; // TODO - If you are not executing the Pay call
                                    // for a preapproval, then you must set a valid
                                    //  cancelUrl for the web approval flow that
                                    // immediately follows this Pay call
$returnUrl = "https://myreturnurl"; // TODO - If you are not executing the Pay call
                                    // for a preapproval, then you must set a valid
                                    // returnUrl for the web approval flow that
                                    // immediately follows this Pay call
$currencyCode = "USD";

// A chained payment can be made with 1 primary receiver and between 1 and 5 secondary
// receivers
// TODO - Specify the receiver emails
//        Remove or set to an empty string the array entries for receivers that you
//        do not have
$receiverEmailArray = array(
  'receiver0email',
  'receiver1email',
  'receiver2email',
  'receiver3email',
  'receiver4email',
  'receiver5email'
  );

// TODO - Specify the receiver amounts as the amount of money, for example, '5' or '5.55'
//        Remove or set to an empty string the array entries for receivers that you
//        do not have
$receiverAmountArray = array(
  'receiver0amount',
  'receiver1amount',
  'receiver2amount',
  'receiver3amount',
  'receiver4amount',
  'receiver5amount'
  );
```

```
// TODO - Set ONLY 1 receiver in the array to 'true' as the primary receiver, and set the
//        other receivers corresponding to those indicated in receiverEmailArray to
//        'false'. Make sure that you do NOT specify more values in this array than
//        in the receiverEmailArray.
$receiverPrimaryArray = array(
  '',
  '',
  '',
  '',
  '',
  '',
  '',
);

// TODO - Set invoiceId to uniquely identify the transaction associated with each receiver
//        Set the array entries with value for receivers that you have each of the array
//        Values must be unique across all Pay calls made by the caller's API credentials
$receiverInvoiceIdArray = array(
  '',
  '',
  '',
  '',
  '',
  '',
  '',
);

// Request specific optional fields
//    Provide a value for each field that you want to include in the request;
//    if left as an empty string, the field will not be passed in the request
$senderEmail = ""; // TODO - If you are executing the Pay call against a preapprovalKey,
                   // you should set senderEmail
                   // It is not required if the web approval flow immediately
                   // follows this Pay call
$feesPayer = "";
$ipnNotificationUrl = "";
$memo = ""; // maxlength is 1000 characters
$pin = ""; // TODO - If you are executing the Pay call against an existing preapproval
           // that requires a pin, then you must set this
$preapprovalKey = ""; // TODO - If you are executing the Pay call against an existing
                      // preapproval, set the preapprovalKey here
$reverseAllParallelPaymentsOnError = ""; // TODO - Do not specify for chained payment
$trackingId = generateTrackingID(); // generateTrackingID function is found
                                    // in paypalplatform.php

//-------------------------------------------------
// Make the Pay API call
//
// The CallPay function is defined in the paypalplatform.php file,
// which is included at the top of this file.
//-------------------------------------------------
$resArray = CallPay ($actionType, $cancelUrl, $returnUrl, $currencyCode,
    $receiverEmailArray, $receiverAmountArray, $receiverPrimaryArray,
    $receiverInvoiceIdArray, $feesPayer, $ipnNotificationUrl, $memo,
    $pin, $preapprovalKey, $reverseAllParallelPaymentsOnError,
    $senderEmail, $trackingId
);
```

```php
$ack = strtoupper($resArray["responseEnvelope.ack"]);
if($ack=="SUCCESS")
{
 if ("" == $preapprovalKey)
 {
  // redirect for web approval flow
  $cmd = "cmd=_ap-payment&paykey=" . urldecode($resArray["payKey"]);
  RedirectToPayPal ( $cmd );
 }
 else
 {
  // The Pay API call was made for an existing preapproval agreement, so no approval
  // flow follows.
  // payKey is the key that you can use to identify the result from this Pay call.
  $payKey = urldecode($resArray["payKey"]);
  // paymentExecStatus is the status of the payment
  $paymentExecStatus = urldecode($resArray["paymentExecStatus"]);
  // Note that in order to get the exact status of the transactions resulting from
  // a Pay API call, you should make the PaymentDetails API call for the payKey
 }
}
else
{
 //Display a user-friendly Error on the page using any of the following error information
 //returned by PayPal.
 //TODO - There can be more than 1 error, so check for "error(1).errorId",
 //       then "error(2).errorId", and so on until you find no more errors.
 $ErrorCode = urldecode($resArray["error(0).errorId"]);
 $ErrorMsg = urldecode($resArray["error(0).message"]);
 $ErrorDomain = urldecode($resArray["error(0).domain"]);
 $ErrorSeverity = urldecode($resArray["error(0).severity"]);
 $ErrorCategory = urldecode($resArray["error(0).category"]);

 echo "Pay API call failed. ";
 echo "Detailed Error Message: " . $ErrorMsg;
 echo "Error Code: " . $ErrorCode;
 echo "Error Severity: " . $ErrorSeverity;
 echo "Error Domain: " . $ErrorDomain;
 echo "Error Category: " . $ErrorCategory;
}
?>
```

CHAPTER 5

PayPal Mobile Express Checkout

The latest wave of development focuses on creating applications and commerce interfaces for the mobile market. At the Innovate 2010 Developer Conference, PayPal announced the release of Mobile Express Checkout (MEC), which is built on the existing Express Checkout API. Mobile Express Checkout allows for fast development, especially if you already have an Express Checkout-based solution. In addition to Mobile Express Checkout, PayPal provides development libraries, or Mobile Payment Libraries (MPL), for both the iPhone and Android platforms. Table 5-1, also provided by Bill Day at *https://www.x.com/docs/DOC-3035*, outlines the standard PayPal APIs and their mobile equivalents.

Table 5-1. Standard PayPal APIs and mobile equivalents

PayPal APIs you use today	Use this for native mobile development	Use this for mobile web development
Express Checkout	MEC library for iOS	MEC
Adaptive Payments	MPL	N/A
Website Payments Standard	MPL	N/A

MPL is a native application development option, and it is especially useful if you are targeting apps on iOS- or Android-based devices that have no backend commerce infrastructure to interface with. MPL also supports some PayPal technologies currently not addressed by MEC, such as Adaptive Payments.

To fully utilize the capabilities of Mobile Express Checkout and the development libraries, you should be familiar with mobile website programming, the Name-Value Pair API, and additionally the platform you are developing on if integrating with a mobile application. It should also be noted that iOS uses Objective-C, and so knowledge of this language is a plus. Let's look at the MEC flow first.

Mobile Express Checkout Flow

The MEC flow, shown in Figure 5-1, has the following steps:

1. The customer clicks the "Checkout with PayPal" button on your site.
2. The customer logs into PayPal.
3. The customer reviews the transaction on PayPal and submits payment.
4. The customer receives an order confirmation.

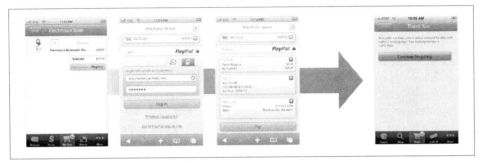

Figure 5-1. Mobile Express Checkout flow

As you can see, Mobile Express Checkout functions identically to Express Checkout, but MEC has several design and implementation best practices to consider, which are outlined next.

Mobile Express Checkout Best Practices

Just as with Express Checkout, shortcut placement for MEC is key. Customers can enter into MEC from either the Shopping Cart (where users see the items they are purchasing) or the Payments page (where they are asked to provide all their billing and payment information). The recommendations and requirements when entering from the Shopping Cart are as follows:

- "Checkout with PayPal" buttons should be used.
- You must use approved, hosted PayPal buttons.
- You cannot resize any PayPal-supplied images.
- The checkout button should take the customer directly to PayPal.
- It should take no more then two pages after the PayPal pages to complete the payment.
- The recommended flows are Shopping Cart→Login→Review→Confirmation, or Shopping Cart→Login→Review→Additional Review with Submit→Confirmation.

If you are entering into MEC from the Payments page, the recommendations and requirements are as follows:

- The PayPal Payment Mark should be used.
- You must use approved, hosted PayPal marks.
- You cannot resize any PayPal-supplied images.
- Radio buttons should have at least a 44 pixel spacing to enable easy selection on touch-enabled devices.

If your customer has already set up a billing agreement through Express Checkout online, the "Checkout with PayPal" button should contain her email address. Doing so helps to personalize the transaction. If there is no billing agreement set up, the basic "Checkout with PayPal" button should be used.

Mobile Express Checkout Library for iOS

PayPal provides a MEC library for iOS, available for download from *https://www.x.com/community/ppx/xspaces/mobile/mobile_ec*. This MEC library supports two different programming flows: it can be called either directly from your mobile application or via a PayPal button on your mobile website.

MEC Mobile Application Integration

MEC can be integrated into your mobile application, allowing you to start and end the payment process with screens inside your application. The MEC checkout pages themselves are contained inside a web view. The steps for doing so are as follows:

1. Acquire a device token from the MEC library before rendering the payment screen with the PayPal Button. Include a pointer to the method you delegate for handling the device token.
2. Acquire a PayPal payment button from the Library and render it on your mobile application screen. Include a pointer to the method you delegate for handling the button-click event.
3. When your customer clicks the PayPal button, it will initialize your delegated method to do the following:
   a. Call a routine on your mobile web server for passing the payment information.
   b. Your mobile web server will then send a SetExpressCheckout request with the payment information to PayPal.
   c. Pass the checkout token returned from SetExpressCheckout back to your mobile application.

d. Open a web view redirecting the customer's browser to PayPal with the `Mobile` command, using the device token and the checkout token as URL parameters. For example:

```
https://www.paypal.com/cgi-bin/webscr?cmd=_express-checkout-mobile
&drt=valueFromMobileExpressCheckoutLibrary&token=valueFromSetExpres
sCheckoutResponse
```

e. Watch the web view for a redirect call from PayPal to either your return or cancel URLs.

f. If PayPal redirects the web view to your return URL, call surrogate routines on your mobile web server that send `GetExpressCheckoutDetails` and `DoExpressCheckoutPayment` requests to PayPal to complete the payment.

MEC Mobile Website Integration

MEC can be integrated directly with your mobile website, allowing you to start and end the payment process with pages on your site. The steps for doing so are as follows:

1. Acquire a device token from the MEC library before rendering the web view of your MEC implementation. Include a pointer to the method you delegate for handling the device token.

2. Launch a web view of the web page or routine on your mobile server that initiates your checkout process. Include the device token as a URL parameter, as well as the item details in the shopping cart.

3. Watch the web view for a redirect from your mobile web server that contains a call to a known URL, signaling the checkout process is complete.

MEC Library Methods

MEC contains three methods: `fetchDeviceReferenceTokenWithAppID`, `getPayButtonWithTarget`, and `getInstance`. Let's look at each in depth.

fetchDeviceReferenceTokenWithAppID method

The `fetchDeviceReferenceTokenWithAppID` method returns a device token for use with the transaction. Use the `del` parameter to specify your delegate function that receives device tokens. Device tokens have a 45-minute expiration time limit, and are passed as the `&drt` parameter on the URL when you redirect the mobile browser to PayPal.

The MEC library uses the PayPal production servers by default to get device tokens. During your development process, use the `env` parameter to fetch device tokens from the sandbox. Be sure to fetch the device token just before you get the PayPal button. When you fetch the device token, the library determines whether the buyer stays logged in on the device. If the buyer is already logged into PayPal, the library will display the buyer's name above the button when it renders. Table 5-2 outlines the parameters for fetchDeviceReferenceTokenWithAppID.

Table 5-2. fetchDeviceReferenceTokenWithAppID method

Parameter	Description
inAppId:	The PayPal Application ID from X.com (required). For the sandbox environment, use APP-80W284485P519543T.
env:	Indicates which PayPal servers the library uses (optional). Allowable values are:
	• ENV_LIVE
	• ENV_SANDBOX
	• ENV_NONE
del:	Your delegate function that receives device tokens (required).

getPayButtonWithTarget method

If your payment implementation is in a mobile application, you can get a button from the MEC library. The getPayButtonWithTarget method returns a UIButton for use on your mobile application screen, and it provides a target: parameter that allows you to specify which UIViewController receives the callbacks. Table 5-3 outlines the parameters for getPayButtonWithTarget.

Table 5-3. getPayButtonWithTarget method

Parameter	Description
target:	The UIViewController that is the delegate for callbacks (required).
action:	Your method that responds to the PayPal button click (required).
buttonType:	The size and appearance of the PayPal button (required). Allowable values are:
	• BUTTON_152x33
	• BUTTON_194x37
	• BUTTON_278x43
	• BUTTON_294x43

getInstance method

You can use the getInstance method to specify and access the library's runtime properties. This can be used for debugging purposes as well as to verify that your payment is working properly. Table 5-4 outlines the parameters for getInstance.

Table 5-4. getInstance method

Parameter	Description
lang	The locale code for the label of the PayPal button. By default, the library uses the locale of the device.
errorMessage	If the library fails to acquire a valid device token, the error message provides more details about the failure.
paymentsEnabled	If your attempt to fetch a device token succeeded, the value of this property is TRUE.

MEC Localization Support

MEC supports numerous locales, which can be specified after you initialize the library. By default it will determine the local of the user's device, and if it does not support the device's locale, it will fall back on en_US. You specify the locale with the `lang` property of the PayPal object. This should be set after initializing the library and before you make the call to `getPayButtonWithTarget()` to get a localized button. Table 5-5 lists the supported localizations.

Table 5-5. Supported localizations

Country or region	Supported locale codes
Argentina	es_AR
Brazil	pt_BR
Australia	en_AU
Belgium	en_BE, nl_BR, fr_BE
Canada	en_CA, fr_CA
France	fr_FR, en_FR
Germany	de_DE, en_DE
Hong Kong	zh_HK, en_HK
India	en_IN
Italy	it_IT
Japan	ja_JP, en_JP
Mexico	es_MX, en_MX
Netherlands	nl_NL, en_NL
Poland	pl_PL, en_PL
Singapore	en_SG
Spain	es_ES, en_ES
Switzerland	de_CH, en_CH, fr_CH
Taiwan	zh_TW, en_TW
United States	en_US

Sample MEC Code

The MEC library includes a library header file, *PayPal.h*, for your mobile application or mobile web code. The contents of *PayPal.h* are shown in Example 5-1. You can access features of the MEC library using the "PayPal : NSObject <UIWebViewDelegate>" interface.

Example 5-1. PayPal.h

```
#import <UIKit/UIKit.h>


typedef enum PayPalEnvironment {
 ENV_LIVE,
 ENV_SANDBOX,
 ENV_NONE,
} PayPalEnvironment;

typedef enum PayPalButtonType {
 BUTTON_118x24,
 BUTTON_152x33,
 BUTTON_194x37,
 BUTTON_278x43,
 BUTTON_294x43,
 BUTTON_TYPE_COUNT,
}PayPalButtonType;

@protocol DeviceReferenceTokenDelegate <NSObject>

@required
- (void)receivedDeviceReferenceToken:(NSString *)token;
- (void)couldNotFetchDeviceReferenceToken; //Check the errorMessage property to see what
                                 //the problem was.

@end


@interface PayPal : NSObject <UIWebViewDelegate> {
 @private
 BOOL initialized;//Determines if the initialization call has finished and the PayPal
                //object is initialized.
 BOOL paymentsEnabled;
 NSString *appID;
 NSString *lang;
 PayPalEnvironment environment;

 NSString *errorMessage;
 NSMutableArray *payButtons;

 id<DeviceReferenceTokenDelegate> delegate;
}
```

```
@property (nonatomic, retain) NSString *lang;
@property (nonatomic, retain) NSString *errorMessage;
@property (nonatomic, retain) NSMutableArray *payButtons;

@property (nonatomic, readonly) NSString *appID;
@property (nonatomic, readonly) BOOL initialized;
@property (nonatomic, readonly) BOOL paymentsEnabled;
@property (nonatomic, readonly) PayPalEnvironment environment;

+ (PayPal*)getInstance;

- (void)fetchDeviceReferenceTokenWithAppID:(NSString const *)
inAppID forEnvironment:(PayPalEnvironment)env
withDelegate:(id<DeviceReferenceTokenDelegate>)del;
- (void)fetchDeviceReferenceTokenWithAppID:(NSString const *)
inAppID withDelegate:(id<DeviceReferenceTokenDelegate>)del;

- (UIButton *)getPayButtonWithTarget:(NSObject const *)target andAction:(SEL)action
andButtonType:(PayPalButtonType)inButtonType;

@end
```

A full example of using the MEC library for an online pizza delivery service application can be found in the library download at *https://www.x.com/community/ppx/xspaces/mobile/mobile_ec*.

Summary

MEC is a new PayPal offering, but it builds on the tried and true PayPal Express Checkout. PayPal continues to bring new technologies into the realm of payment solutions. In this book, I've tried to provide the fundamental knowledge you need to choose which PayPal solution is right for you and understand how to implement that solution into your unique situation. I hope that I have succeeded in both of these avenues.

Index

We'd like to hear your suggestions for improving our indexes. Send email to *index@oreilly.com*.

About the Author

Michael Balderas started his technology career in 1995 in Fort Worth, Texas, with hardware and Internet services. He began his transition to database architecture and utility interfaces in 1996. Over the years, Mike has expanded his skills to include frontend and middleware development. One of his most notable projects is the architecture of an enterprise suite for the law enforcement and homeland security marketplace, which has been lauded by the Director of the FBI and the Secretary of Homeland Security. Mike enjoys designing and developing technology that delivers a seamless integration with people and processes for optimal results.

Colophon

The animal on the cover of *PayPal APIs: Up and Running* is an African wildcat (*Felis silvestris cafra*), also known as a desert cat or African caffre. Studies suggest that the common domesticated cat is yet another subspecies of *Felis silvestris* and that the cats domesticated themselves around 10,000 years ago in the Middle East. As agriculture developed in ancient civilizations, humans began to store large amounts of grain. These granaries attracted rodents, and in turn, wildcats.

Thus, the African wildcat bears a resemblance to domesticated cats, though it is roughly 1.5 times larger at 18–30 inches long and 7–14 pounds. Among their population, these animals are also much more similar in appearance to each other than house cats. Their coats range from sandy brown to gray, with a white belly and black stripes on the legs and tail. They have shorter fur and are smaller than the main wildcat species of Europe.

The African wildcat can be found throughout sub-Saharan Africa, and another African subspecies (*F. s. lybica*) ranges through northern Africa and the Middle East. These animals live in a variety of habitats, such as grasslands and forests. They primarily hunt at night, catching mice and other small mammals, as well as birds, reptiles, and amphibians if the opportunity arises. During the day, they rest in concealed places like old burrows or thick vegetation.

Unsurprisingly, wildcats share many behaviors with domestic felines, such as burying their droppings and vocalizing with purrs, yowls, meows, and hisses. Their genetic similarities may pose a threat to the African wildcat, however; in areas where there is a wildcat population living near human settlements, it is common for wild and domestic cats to interbreed. It is now difficult to find purebred African wildcats anywhere near civilization, which may not bode well for it remaining a unique species.

The cover image is from Lydekker's *Royal Natural History*. The cover font is Adobe ITC Garamond. The text font is Linotype Birka; the heading font is Adobe Myriad Condensed; and the code font is LucasFont's TheSansMonoCondensed.

Get even more for your money.

Register the O'Reilly books you own, and you'll receive:

Special offers
Get special offers and discounts available only to registered O'Reilly customers.

Discounts on new editions
Receive email notification and special discounts on new editions of your registered O'Reilly books.

Your personal online inventory of the O'Reilly books you own
Keep track of your O'Reilly library.

Free stuff
Win free books, t-shirts, and other O'Reilly gear.

Registering your books is easy:
1. **Go to: oreilly.com/go/register**
2. **Create an O'Reilly login.**
3. **Provide your address.**
4. **Register your books.**

Note: English-language books only

To order books online:
oreilly.com/order_new

For questions about products or an order:
orders@oreilly.com

To sign up to get topic-specific email announcements and/or news about upcoming books, conferences, special offers, and new technologies:
elists@oreilly.com

For technical questions about book content:
booktech@oreilly.com

To submit new book proposals to our editors:
proposals@oreilly.com

Many O'Reilly books are available in PDF and several ebook formats. For more information:
oreilly.com/ebooks

Spreading the knowledge of innovators   www.oreilly.com

The information you need, when and where you need it.

With Safari Books Online, you can:

Access the contents of thousands of technology and business books

- Quickly search over 7000 books and certification guides
- Download whole books or chapters in PDF format, at no extra cost, to print or read on the go
- Copy and paste code
- Save up to 35% on O'Reilly print books
- **New!** Access mobile-friendly books directly from cell phones and mobile devices

Stay up-to-date on emerging topics before the books are published

- Get on-demand access to evolving manuscripts.
- Interact directly with authors of upcoming books

Explore thousands of hours of video on technology and design topics

- Learn from expert video tutorials
- Watch and replay recorded conference sessions

O'REILLY®